"Priceless and transformati
let go of painful shame bec
your relationship to food th.. ,ᴏᴜ ..eeᴅ to read *Too Big for My Britches* by Stacey Hawkins. Her courageous and heartfelt story is uncensored and raw. It gives real words to the feelings experienced alone and in silence and like a distant light of hope she carries us through to the other side. This book will be a tool of change for the scores of women, and frankly men too, who read it. It is life-changing. I only wish I had it as a resource when I counseled so many women who shared a similar story struggling for a similar conclusion."

KEITH LEWIS
Former Executive Director MISS USA (California, New York, New Hampshire)

"Having little time to read anything, I literally could not put down this book! Stacey's story is compelling, real, and raw. Her story is "Everywoman's" story: the climb from believing the lie that we are not enough to pure grit and defiance, which allows us all to believe in our own strength and magnificence. What I wish for each and every girl and young woman growing up is that they learn that there's no such thing as being "too big for our britches" -- that each of us is born to rise to our own greatness. Yes: that we literally DARE to be glorious and fantastic. This is a book I recommend to women - and men - who need to be inspired to live up to their best selves, their highest potential and possibilities. Thank you, Stacey, for giving us a book which inspires and guides others to be their authentic selves!"

SHEILA PEARL
Relationship Coach
Author, *Ageless & Sexy: The Magic of Sensuality*

"As an integrative life coach specializing in helping women understand and remove shame from their bodies, I recognize how a book like this can truly inspire and change lives. Stacey's story is compelling, motivating and is a flame starter to any woman's journey to reclaiming her relationship with food and self-love. She gets what it means to feel "less than" and provides helpful, practical, and loving guidance on breaking through to a happier, more rewarding, and fulfilling life. Bravo!"

PAMELA MADSEN
Sexuality and Relationship Consultant
Seen in the *New York Times*, *Huffington Post*, *Oprah*, and NBC

"As a health and wellness coach that specializes in helping women and mothers, this book is a MUST-read. Why? Because this is not just another diet plan or diet book; in fact, it's not that at all. It's a real-life story and expression of what can happen with a positive mindset and attitude shift. *Too Big For My Britches* is compelling and transparent. Stacey shares how she lost an incredible amount of weight and used this battle to change her life and inspire others to do the same. Her story will make you laugh, cry, and feel empowered. After reading this book, it's clear that Stacey lost the weight, but her journey allowed her to gain so much more—self-worth. For anyone struggling with weight loss, body issues, or simply a lack of self-confidence, this book will not only get you excited to make positive changes but to jump on a treadmill, whip up some healthy meals, and start loving yourself again."

LIZ CORT
Fitness Professional
Founder, TeamFitMom.com
Owner, Fitness Fusion Studio
Diamond Advocare Coach

TOO BIG

FOR

MY BRITCHES

How I let go of body shame and
became proud of simply being me
(*and how you can too*)

STACEY HAWKINS

Storehouse Publishing, LLC

St. Augustine, Florida

Too Big for My Britches
How I let Go of Body Shame and Became Proud of Simply Being Me (and How You Can Too)

Storehouse Publishing, LLC
Saint Augustine, Florida 32092
www.StorehousePublishers.com
Author@StorehousePublishers.com

Ordering Information:
Quantity sales. Special discounts are available on quantity purchases by corporations, associations, and others. For details, contact the "Special Sales Department" with the Publisher at the email address above and type in subject line "Special Sales Department."

The views expressed in this work are solely those of the author and do not necessarily reflect the views of the publisher, and the publisher hereby disclaims any responsibility for them.

Cover design by Dave Humphrey
Book design and production by Storehouse Publishing, LLC
Editing by Sherrie Clark at www.TheAuthorShip.net
Author photograph by Renee Parenteau.

Too Big for My Britches / Stacey Hawkins. —1st ed.

ISBN-10:   1-943106-05-3 (sc)
ISBN-13:   978-1-943106-05-9 (sc)
ISBN-10:   1-943106-06-1 (ebk)
ISBN-13:   978-1-943106-06-6 (ebk)

Library of Congress Control Number: 2016903699

Printed in the United States of America

DEDICATION

For Chase, Jacqueline,
T.C.,
Mom and Dad.
I love you all.

Epigraph

The mind is incessantly looking not only for food for thought;
it is also looking for food for its identity,
its sense of self.
This is how the ego comes into existence and
continuously re-creates itself.

—ECKHART TOLLE

DISCLAIMER

This book is not intended as a substitute for the medical advice of physicians. The reader should regularly consult a physician in matters relating to his/her health and particularly with respect to any symptoms that may require diagnosis or medical attention.

I have tried to recreate events, locales, and conversations from my memories of them. In order to maintain their anonymity in some instances, I have changed the names of individuals and places. I may have changed some identifying characteristics and details, such as physical properties, occupations, and places of residence.

Although the author and publisher have made every effort to ensure that the information in this book was correct at press time, the author and publisher do not assume and hereby disclaim any liability to any party for any loss, damage, or disruption caused, or alleged to have been caused, directly or indirectly, by errors or omissions, whether such errors or omissions result from negligence, accident, or any other cause, by the information in this book.

ACKNOWLEDGEMENTS

This book could not have been written without the vast number of people in my life who have influenced me in one way, shape, or form. The profound experiences we shared, whether they're for a moment or a lifetime, led me on this incredible journey. I do hope I have remembered you all.

First and foremost, I'd like to acknowledge my family. I never would have had the inspiration to create this work without you: my children Chase and Jacqueline Hawkins (who rocks more than the two of you?). I am more proud of you than you will ever know. To my parents Robert and Marsha Horner, who did their best to bring me up in this world, loving and motivating me every day; my brother Scott Horner for the decades of constant little-brother "entertainment." I'm so proud (and kind of surprised, LOL) of how cool you turned out to be, and for his wife Lindsay and kids Grant and Gavin; my Baba Martha Perzel, who founded my love of cooking; my great-grandmother Gladys Horner, who inspired me to be a strong and unashamed woman in business; my cousins Tracy (and her husband Mark), Beth and Lindsay Perzel, who stood by me and reassured me that I was far from crazy (OMG, TY!); my Aunt Ruthanne and Uncle George Perzel, who continue to support and encourage my business ideas; my cousin Barbara Gonzales, who inspired my quest for health and helping others; my Aunt Corrine Pacelli and her children Celeste and A.J, my Aunt

Beverly and Uncle Hank Malitsky and their children Kristin and Kara for the hard lessons learned; and my grandfather Robert W. Horner whose memory motivates me daily to live a life of no regrets.

I'd especially like to thank Joseph W. Potyak, Jr., a man who says few words but speaks volumes through his actions and especially his hugs. Thank you for being my brick wall covered in pillows. Simply being in the moment with you, wherever adventures may take us, makes me feel happier than ever. My existence changed forever for the better the day you entered our lives. I'd also like to thank his children Samantha and Matthew for allowing me to see that being a "mom" can happen in many ways. I love you all.

This book would have never come to be if not for the inspiration and belief of Dave Humphrey and his powerhouse talent at SLR: Tammie, Gabe, and Abby. I am forever grateful for the motivation and for each of you for helping me truly shine.

Also to Sherrie Clark, my editor extraordinaire! Your skill is much more than grammatically correct, and your patience with me seems to know no boundaries. I am blessed to have worked with all of you.

For my dear friends Justine Lease, Lori Fakler, Michael Pine, Christine Mandoske, Chris Shaw, Heidi Sherwood, Kelly Martineau, Heather Batelic, Danyelle Means, Angelyn Galati, Mary Winn Gordon, Nancy and Rick Brownell, Chris Bromley, Kim Bromley, Michael Settino, Heather Smith Nunez, Michael Smith and Julie Henderson, Shirley Felder, Maria Blon, Jane

Savage, Kristen Cullen, Trish McMullen, Michael and Jennifer Nolan and their family Trisha O'Malley, Amanda, and Peter Merli, Russ and Megan Kasin and their girls, Julie Cestaro, Kristie Brand, Lynne Schlitz, Mark Schlitz, Sara and Drew Uth, and to Josh and Tara Jacobsen and their awesome kids Morgan and Noah.

From my early childhood days, I'd like to recognize friends of the family Celeste and Jack Cornell and their extended posse, especially my bestie, their son David, for the thousands of laughs and shared experiences. Thanks to my family friends Barrie and Peter Sovich and their children Peter and Geoff. Barrie was one of the most influential people in my life and is sorely missed. To my partner in crime, Krista Fabian, and her unwavering enthusiasm to make creative productions of our talents for all to watch. (We should have charged admission). For Len and Marion Fairfield and their children Julie and David, and for my friends Mim and Lisa Pratt and the everlasting memories of laughing with you both that still come to me to this very day when I smell hot fresh-baked bread.

I spent the eighties growing up with the most extreme Motley Crue (pun intended) I could have ever imagined. To my very best friend in the entire world, Christine Brundege, for being my confidant, my friend, and my life raft. I could not have made it without you and your parents Lin and Lynn and your brother Tim. To my amazing mentor, friend, and second mom Emily Adams, who taught me to be true to myself. I regret we never got to say goodbye. To Allison Bayer and her mom Jeanne, who loved us all and made us feel our most confident without question; Sue Solotruck, Rita Greiner, Ramona Papke and her mom Mary Ellen, Sue Thomas, Nancy Ravena, Nicole Mink, Amy Berrigan, Lindy McQueen, Andrea Spensieri, Wendy Lawrence, Dale Delaney, Joanna Reese, Jim Koines, Michele Arndt, Scott Gardner, Stacy Speidel, Stacy Sheehan, Bobby Iovinella, Brian Ettrich, Bob Edmiston, Mike Komar, Terry Jones, Todd Hart, Cindy Heritage, Todd Hunt, Nicole Capasso, Ruth Howansky, Aimee Alexander, Kristie Schlegel, Greg Stevens, and the Carr sisters Kimberly and Amy. Lastly, to Tim Gardner, my first true love, thank you for breaking my heart (really ☺). I had so many adventures with this group, and they made twelve years of school come and go so fast.

From my college and early working years, I'd like to acknowledge Holly Marcille, Alicia Suling, Thea Romano, Angela Varicchio, Jeanne Devaney, Dawn Eldredge, Kerry Henning, Eileen Moran, Penny Law, Wendy and Tom Mc Nutt, Mark Shaw, Mark Domalewski, Chris and Bonnie Algozzine, Alan Labouseur, Barbara Boccuto, and Denise Merritt. Thank you for showing me the ropes and cleaning up after me when necessary. To Trista Polo (and of course Russell too), wow, what can I say except I love you like a sister. Thank you for being there...always.

To Keith Lewis, who needs an entire page for me to give him all the thanks he deserves but will accept these few lines because he knows what's in my heart.

To Cate McCoy for opening new doors and helping me close old ones. Your friendship will remain forever.

To my amazing business support team Patrick DiChiro and his team at Thunderfactory for getting it all started way back when: Eric Egland, Rob Unger, Anna Gibbs, Steven Heller, Esq., Matt Benson, Kellie Shallian and her father Ted O'Lear who restored my faith in good old-fashioned business with humanity and a handshake. I'd also like to heartily thank Roseann Shales, consultant-turned-friend and mentor, for her constant encouragement, enlightenment, unwavering support, and sound advice.

To the wonderful group of men and women who believed in what I was doing and willingly shared their knowledge to help me succeed. I cannot thank you enough: Mr. Morris Golombeck and the team at Golombeck Spices, Jim Denihan, Dave Miller, Yvette Yeomans, Sharon Moyer, The Junior League of Orange County, Aida and Edison Guzman, Michelle Tomasicchio, Gladys and Leonard Bell, Nan and Brian DeGroat, Dr. Wayne Anderson, Dan Van Zandt, Deborah Stillman, Barbara Pagan, Gina Babbage, Liz Cort and her amazing Advocare Team Fuzion, and especially my mentor, friend, and inspiration Paula Martino. I also want to personally thank Deanna Bellacicco for your undying support, for sharing your entrepreneur brain, and of course, for keeping me and the kids supplied with cookies!

To my pleasure-seeking posse Linda Mironti, Noriko Kawamoto, Karen Lewis, Francesqua Darling, Linda Kim Davies, Lisa Slack, Lori Berkowitz, Anna Lisa C. Tempestini, and to my big sister Caroline Davies—mmmmuuuaahh! Thank you for teaching me SO much and for showering me with the beauty of your vulnerability. No matter how many miles are between us, we are forever bonded by church bells. To my friends, mentors, and soul mothers Sheila Pearl and Pamela Madsen. There are no words that could express my heartfelt gratitude for your hugs (and your spanks). Thanks also to the men in this category, most especially Ron Stewart, Neal Wecker, and of course the window tinter for helping unleash my true beauty.

To my delightful culinary team Tama Murphy (OMG, that's all I'm gonna say), Chef Phil Crispo, Chef Mark Ainsworth, Chef John DeShelter, and Andre Rush, I can't thank you enough for so firmly rooting for me when so many didn't. I am thankful for your encouragement, your pushing me to be the best, and for your time and patience.

I would like to thank the entire volunteer team and my fellow classmates at the School of Practical Philosophy in Wallkill, New York. Chris Wood, Earl and Diane Miller, Donald Weigmann, and the whole student body have opened my eyes to more than I could have ever dreamed a few years ago. Thank you for the opportunity to learn and for sharing your knowledge selflessly.

A huge thank you to all of the women, men, and businesses who opened their doors to allow me and/or my team of Strategists into their homes so that we may delight and inspire you and your guests to cook, eat, and live better. Although I didn't have the privilege to meet all of you who hosted these events and the thousands of you who attended, please know how much I appreciate your individual hospitality and willingness to try new things. And to all my customers who have purchased our products, thank you for trusting me to nourish you.

I hold such deep appreciation in my heart for some of the most brave, trusting, and empowering women who believed in me, my mission, and my products enough to step up to the plate and join the very first Stacey Hawkins direct sales team. Your friendship, your feedback, and your support has meant the world to me: Jennifer Nolan, Donna D'Amico, Melanie Potter, Sue Barki, Gina Zwart, Julie Byrnes, Nannette DeGroat, Trish Rogers, Jamie Montanaro, Holly Parker, Tara Jacobsen, Bonnee Clyde, Teri Gross, Lori Perrone, Ann Rettus, Alison Melahn, Cheryl McCartney, Chris Ann Harper, Diana Tome, Robbin Colandrea, Pam Graffam, Sari Medick, Ellen Haspel, Trish Barkman, and Trish Robbins. I humbly and gratefully stand before you and say, "Thank you."

Lastly, I thank YOU for wanting more from your life and for buying this book to help you make it happen. Let's do this!

CONTENTS

INTRODUCTION

I got out of the tub, caught sight of myself in the mirror, and cried. In an instant, all of the luxuriant feelings of care and comfort I had just received from my rejuvenating bath disappeared.

Forcing myself to take a good hard look at my body, I became overcome with emotion, instantly feeling ashamed and sick to my stomach at the image before me. I angrily grabbed my rolls of fat, jiggling them with disgust while furrowing my brow and scrutinizing myself from every angle in the mirror.

Without batting an eyelash, I berated myself, saying some of the most cruel words a new mother could say to herself about the amazing vessel that had only recently and flawlessly pulled off the miracle of birth.

"Oh, gross. I am so fat. Look at this stomach, these arms, this ass! I hate my body. I am so freaking ugly and worthless. I need to stop eating. I just...need...to *stop*...eating. What the hell is wrong with me?"

These harsh words were carbon copies of messages I had told myself my entire life. Starting at a young age, my body shame had become what felt like a life-sentence. Throughout my youth, mixed messages about healthy bodies, self-love, and food seemed everywhere, especially at home.

By the age of ten, I had popped my first diet pill, and the cycle of binging on comfort food and then berating my body began. I started comparing myself to images I saw on television and in magazines and to the girls around me. The bodies I saw were the exact opposite of the impression I had of myself. Perfect bodies, small bodies with flawless skin, no hips, and no boobs and able to wear just about any clothing and look amazing seemed to be everywhere but in my mirror.

I felt inferior and worthless and wanted to hide. My shame would continue for almost three more decades until one day when I decided that I had enough. I wanted to break free from the bonds of body shame, pave a better way, and be a better role model for my children. I decided to make some drastic changes. Little did I know then that this decision would lead me to unlock the most amazing life I could have ever dreamed.

My story is not unique; however, I have discovered along the way to recovery that my happy ending is. After interacting with thousands of people just like you, I have seen firsthand the suffering caused by decades of comparisons and lack of self-acceptance. No matter what individuals believe their imperfections to be, so many still suffer the excruciating pain of body shame and guilt. I wrote this book to try and change all of that.

Through the story of my journey, I have bared it all, literally and figuratively. I have been uncomfortably vulnerable as I have ripped back the veils on what appeared to be a perfect life to the outside world. This full exposure allows you to personally embrace my recipes for freedom from body and food shame so that you can achieve personal happiness, self-acceptance, and most of all, love and understanding.

While reading my story, you will see that you are not alone in your imperfection. You will come to understand what incredible beauty lies in *simply being you* and see that you no longer have to just hope that things can be better; you can take actions right now that can lead you to a whole new life. It's waiting for you.

1
WHAT LITTLE GIRLS ARE MADE OF

"There's no place like home."
—Dorothy, *The Wizard of Oz*

I was only seven years old when I learned my first lesson on how destructively powerful the combination of human emotion and food can be. While I was too young to put words or meaning to what I felt at that time, the experience left a lifelong mark that would carve my painful path over the next four decades. The wounding would continue to play a huge role in almost every major decision I made until that life-changing day when I said, "No more."

It all started in the spring of 1977, when we traveled to my grandmother Baba's house in Hazleton, Pennsylvania, for the annual family Easter feast. My aunts, uncles, cousins, and my immediate family all gathered for food, festivities, and the typical insanity that ensues when such events happen.

Despite the flurry of activity all around, none of them really involved me. I couldn't help but be bored, which understandably caused me to be a bit underfoot. So when I learned that my aunt and her daughter were going on an unexpected preholiday shopping trip and was asked to join them, I eagerly agreed. The events that unfolded during this adventure and afterward would prove to become a common theme in the story of my life.

At the start of the trip, though, everything was fine. I was full of naivety, confidence, and excitement. Even the overcast skies did nothing to alter my enthusiasm, and I hastily bounced out of the car as soon as we stopped at *the* premier shoe store in downtown Hazleton.

My Auntie B, my mother's oldest sister, acquired her customary position as the leader of the pack. She was a woman who ran the roost, not through kindness and respect but through dominating, soul-shattering fear that everyone seemed to experience while in her presence. From the moment she walked into a room, she commanded it in the same way a bully commands a playground. Her face wore a formidable scowl that summed everyone up in a critical and judgmental fashion. No one seemed to pass her inspection as demonstrated by the condescending tone she used when speaking to that person. Make no mistake, Auntie was a master bully and used to getting whatever she wanted. Heaven help the person who questioned her or got in her way.

She approached the store and pushed her way through the door ready for fierce shopping action, her sharp tongue prepared for battle. She was willing do whatever it took to get the best deal.

My cousin waltzed into the store next, following dutifully second in line behind her mother. A year older and *of course* much wiser, she was a goddess in my eyes, the epitome of sheer perfection that I could never hope to be with her long brown locks of hair and petite stature. Her mother made sure that everyone in the family knew how flawless her daughter was, and no one dared to question otherwise, lest he or she suffer Auntie's wrath.

I brought up the rear, bursting into the store with bright-eyed wonder and all the giddiness expected of a little girl who's swimming in a sea of patent, suede, and high-heeled splendor. Still I managed to keep my excitement in tow since being on my best behavior was a strict requirement. No overt displays of enthusiasm were allowed here. I was simply a guest at this outing, asked only to come along for the ride.

I kept my last-place position, ooh-ing and ahh-ing at the colors, the sparkles, the styles, and the magnificence of it all. Inside I felt a tug of exhilaration combined with the angst of "Look but don't touch" and the ever-looming message "Be a good girl or else." These were lessons my mother instilled in me since the moment I was born. But oh, how hard it was to contain myself. Even at the tender age of seven, I understood and had felt the invincible sense of power one could have when wearing the right shoes on your feet.

I soon found myself lost in a daydream of unattainable sparkly desire. I saw myself as a character in the television series *Charlie's Angels* and wearing wedge sandals, as a guest on *The Love Boat* wearing something beautiful while I sat at Captain Stubing's table, or as Wonder Woman in spiky high-heeled boots.

Auntie caught my daydreaming and immediately jolted me into reality. She laughed at me while her finger sliced through the air, pointing from my head to toes. "You're too clumsy to wear heels, girlie!"

Surely she was right. After all, what would people say?

You see, I was already too tall for my age, a giant among my peers, and I self-consciously towered over what seemed like everyone. I felt awkward and socially inept.

My cousin did nothing to deter these feelings. More than once she glared up at me when I got too close or shared her interest. She took distancing herself from common folks like me seriously, following in her mother's footsteps both literally and figuratively. After all, my aunt had worked hard to ensure that everyone knew her family was superior, and she had passed onto her daughter her persona and belief that they were better than everyone else. It was an unwritten rule but clearly understood by anyone who crossed their paths.

For the time being, though, all of the department-store euphoria blissfully distracted my constant feeling of awkwardness and worthlessness around both of them.

When it was my cousin's turn to try on shoes, I sat in a nearby chair where my feet easily touched the ground. While Auntie bossed around the young gentleman clerk, who ran back and forth to the stockroom in an obvious effort to please my cousin, I fidgeted with jealousy and anxiety. I so much wanted the attention lavished upon my cousin, yet I felt quite nervous knowing I needed to please my aunt and meet her expectations with my behavior.

On the clerk's final trip back to the fitting chair, my heart stopped. I watched as the now-cowering shoe man removed the box lid in what appeared to be super-slow motion. I swear I heard horns blaring and saw bright lights shining as he lifted the lid and unveiled the most beautiful pair of red, shiny, patent-leather Mary Jane's you have ever seen. I think I gasped. My cousin did as well as she sat with Cinderella glee while he slipped the sleek red shoe on her foot.

As she claimed those shoes for her own, my heart sank with envy, disappointment, and worthlessness, none of which I could understand at that age. Although young, I was quite able to grasp that the shoes were obviously too good for me since they were being bought for my cousin. After all, who was I to deserve anything so grand?

Upon proceeding to the checkout, Auntie grabbed me hard by the arm and dragged me back to the spot where only moments before glory had been snatched out of my grasp. She plopped me down in the chair and gruffly barked over her shoulder at the timorous clerk while looking me square in the eyes. "Measure fatso's gigantic foot, and go get her a pair too."

I was so taken aback that I froze.

My mind spun with confusion as my little brain became a jumble of shame and excitement. On one hand, I felt humiliated hearing the words "fatso" and "gigantic" come out of my Aunt's mouth as she described me. On the other, I was delirious because I was also getting the shoes. The magnificent light that had radiated from the box only moments before had now transformed into a bolt of lightning.

We returned to my Baba's house, which was now crowded with friends and family and overflowing with the decadent aromas made by the preparations of a traditional Polish Easter dinner. My mother and my Baba were in the kitchen masterfully creating luscious potatoes, flour and butter pancakes, hams, soups, Polish pastries, fruit cookies, sweets, and homemade breads galore. Her tiny, crowded kitchen full of pots, pans, and utensils became a warm, welcoming refuge that I so badly needed in my time of despair.

Half-heartedly I placed the bag that held my new shoes on the table and sat down with a thud. The women sensed something wasn't right. They looked at me and cocked their heads. Their brows furrowed together in confusion.

My mother asked, "Well, how did it go?"

I couldn't hold back any longer. I turned to them both, the inner edges of my eyebrows raised as I sought reassurance and validation. With all of the courage a young girl could muster, I retold the story, sharing my anger and hurt at being called fatso and the humiliation I felt. The tears streamed freely down my face.

My mother had been a seasoned veteran of Bully Auntie B, having quailed to her older sister all her life. Yet she refused to defend me.

She placed her hands on her hips and angrily lashed back at me. "You have no right to say such mean things about your auntie after she just bought you beautiful shoes."

My diminutive, soft, and usually jovial Baba interjected right alongside my mother, but this time, her squeaky voice was stern. Hearing her speak to me in such an angry tone surprised me.

With one hand she wagged her wooden spoon in my face, chastising me while simultaneously slipping a plate of piping-hot, freshly fried, sugar-glazed Long John donuts in front of me with the other hand. "Watch that mouth, missy. You're too darn big for your britches."

They both then turned back to the stove, leaving me ignored and thus dismissed.

Defeated, too young to defend myself when no one else would, and realizing I had nowhere else to turn, I just remained there in stunned silence. I knew nothing good could come from trying to stick up for myself.

My tears silently fell like salty raindrops coating the sweet donuts. Although I didn't know it at the time, but what I had experienced was being shamed, deeply shamed. During this incident, my impressionable and vulnerable brain became flooded with negative images and feelings, and I was force-fed the belief that I and my body were *bad*. Everything from my height to my weight to the size of my feet had been attacked without conscience by influential adults, and I believed every word.

I desperately needed comfort and validation and to make the pain of being *so bad* go away. I also wanted to be a bit rebellious. I picked up one donut after the other and quickly devoured the whole plate, every delicious bite of love cradling me softly in warm, soothing, gooey hugs. Every piece of sugary fried dough, kissed with my salty tears, reassured me that everything was going to be okay. The sweet and the salt played on my tongue without a care. In truth, I ate mindlessly as I simply went numb.

I felt comforted knowing that donuts don't judge. They didn't tell me I was wrong or that I was a bad girl. Eating them was pleasurable. Eating them felt delicious. Eating them felt good when nothing else did.

As soon as the donuts were gone, I did feel better in some ways, but I felt worse in others. Even as a kid, I knew deep down that I shouldn't have eaten *all* of them. After consuming all of those calories, all of that fat, all of that sugar, I felt *huge*, and I felt ashamed, and I scolded myself for my actions. Right there at an impressionable age, the cycle of self-berating began because on that day, my only solace had been a plate of donuts. No one around me seemed to understand my plight, so I sought refuge where I could find it.

Those messages of self-loathing resonated and stayed buried deep in my subconscious brain for decades. No matter what I did, I was just a bad person housed in a bad body. It wasn't that I had actually *done* anything bad; I was simply *bad* at the core of my being, less than, inadequate, completely imperfect, not worthy, and utterly deficient. Oh yeah, let's not forget *huge*. It was what I heard, what I believed, and ultimately what I struggled to change for years.

Rolling Donuts Gather No Moss

Like any "fix," the sweet love of a donut was but a temporary distraction. Although the taste had long faded from my lips, the pain and hurt from the cruel messages that I continually fed myself about being worthless and bad remained.

For years afterward, I felt the effects of just how deep those emotions go when a tender brain/ego/psyche like mine (and so many others) is forced to use harmful coping mechanisms. In my case, I continued to overeat for decades and then beat myself up repeatedly, all in my attempts to find love and acceptance and that sense of "being enough."

Those donuts turned into cookies, and then when I grew up and my budget increased, they turned into luxurious high-end dining and outlandish dinners with friends. As the weight crept up, I tried to be proactive and get control of my weight and eating.

Year after year I'd say, "This time I'll do it," only to fall off the bandwagon again. This turned into even more guilt and shame with countless unused gym memberships, quickly discarded New Years' resolutions, and failed promises I had made to myself.

As a child I could settle for donuts and food in the search for fulfillment, but as an adult I tried to fill in the self-worth void in other ways, especially when food was not enough. I not only dealt with uncontrollable eating binges, alcohol abuse, bad relationships, divorce, and unfulfilling sex, but I became a workaholic and perfectionist as well.

I strived to be the perfect college student, the perfect bride, the perfect wife, and then the perfect mother. This led me to kick myself each time I failed to attain perfection, especially with my body. I tried every diet in the quest for self-acceptance, love, and self-satisfaction. Nothing ever seemed to work. My unresolved problems of not being able to lose weight and feeling unfulfilled kept growing larger and larger... and so did I.

Through it all, the haunting words of *be a good girl or else* still echoed through my head. My number-one mission was to make sure my life looked perfect to the outside world, but I was completely falling apart.

Professionally, I stayed in high-powered stressful jobs that I thought would make my family and me proud. Achievement was everything, so I needed to keep doing, doing, doing.

I couldn't sit still because I was taught that idle time was wasted time. Everything I did had to be *meaningful*. I became the hamster in the wheel, spinning faster and faster with no direction, no goals, and no future. I had no way of knowing at the time that I was whirling with no end in sight. I simply felt I needed to keep moving.

Knowing Better Then Doing Better

All of this ongoing self-destructive behavior stemmed from the simple, harmful words I had heard and believed so long ago, and they had dripped like poison into my mouth. These words weren't reflective of who I really was; they belonged to those adults around me, but I *believed* them. I didn't know any better. That one fateful day in my Baba's kitchen changed everything.

Did my family *mean* to cause long-lasting harm? With the exception of Auntie B, I don't think so. I truly believe that my mother and my grandmother were simply following in the footsteps of the generations of women before them. Sending and receiving mixed and many times toxic messages about food, love, body image, and self-esteem have been the curse of women (and to a lesser extent men) for centuries.

Our mothers, our grandmothers, and on and on down the generational line of women before them have been unknowing victims. They have believed and gone on to share the shameful, confusing ideas and ideals as to whom we are to be and how we are to look, act, and to serve.

Throughout the years we have learned just how much we are to sacrifice ourselves, our wants, our needs, and our desires in order to achieve *perfection*. We are to keep trying and keep berating ourselves until we find it. When we are unsuccessful at doing so, we are to cover up our imperfections.

We're encouraged to become bystanders in our own lives and to play small. We're told that we better not be too big for our britches, either in actual size (by being overweight) or in theory (by shining our lights too brightly) or both. Yet deep down we long to be free from the bonds of imperfection and to live happy and joyous lives. We simply yearn for so much more, often in silence.

Through our daily lives, we receive messages from the outside world that confuse, hurt, and degrade us. Worse yet, we truly believe the hype telling us that we must attain perfection and feel worthless unless we do.

When we have a hard time achieving those results, we feel miserable. We tell *ourselves* over and over that we're not good enough and that we, well, suck. We are our own worst enemies. Truthfully, if we talked to our friends the way we talk to ourselves, we wouldn't have many friends, *if any.*

We think something is wrong with us and that at our core we are lacking, deficient, and not enough. We believe we're not good enough mothers, lovers, and wives. We're not pretty enough, not skinny enough, and not smart enough. We're told we're not taking good enough care of ourselves, our husbands, and our children. *And we believe it.*

This behavior and belief system are damaging. They're crippling. They're ruining our lives, our friends' lives, our daughters' lives, and our mothers' lives. They are destroying our relationships with men, our relationships with our community, and in many cases, they have totally corrupted our relationships with ourselves. They must stop.

We are not the bad people we convince ourselves we are. We are wonderful. We are delicious. We are powerful, strong, and so much more than we ever can imagine. We just need to find our way out of the old beliefs and come into new beliefs of worthiness, love, and acceptance.

But how do we *get* to that place where we feel we are enough? What is the "magic bullet" that allows us to get out of our own way so that we can see the light at the end of the tunnel? What allows us to let go of all the negativity? How do we get empowered? How can we *feel* like better mothers, better daughters, better lovers, and better friends?

The good news is that the act of doing this is simple. Executing it will take some effort, though. You'll need to acknowledge the old feelings and create new ones. You'll need to be willing to accept that everything you know may be false, and you'll need an even bigger willingness to want to change. It won't happen overnight, but I can promise you, *it can happen.* Feeling better all starts with the awareness that the "rules" may not be what you think and then making the simple decision to *break free* from the status quo and let go, opening yourself to a whole new life.

We must make the decision that we are, in fact, *not* those things that we and society have led ourselves to believe. To feel better, you must simply decide that you *are* actually *already* better than you believe. You have that power, and you can harness it. We all can. I'm living proof that it can be done.

I woke up one day and made a deliberate decision that *that* day would be different. I decided that no matter what anyone else ever said, I *would* be enough, enough in my eyes, enough to make *me* happy, and enough to bring me joy, happiness, and peace. The quality of that resolution and each one I have made after that has determined the quality of the new life I am now living for myself. Just like that one day in my Baba's kitchen that negatively affected my life as a child and stayed with me for decades, the decision that allowed me to revamp my old beliefs as an adult changed everything moving forward, and I have never looked back.

In the deliberate blink of an eye, I realized I could actually *be enough.* When I figured out how to reach this goal and overcome all of the challenges and pain from my past, I knew I had something with tremendous value to share with the world.

That is the reason this book is in your hands. Now you have the power to make the decision to be enough too.

2
FOOD, GLORIOUS FOOD

"No, no, go away, I hate you!
And yet... I find you strangely attractive."
—Dark Helmet, *Spaceballs*

I had to hit rock bottom before I had enough motivation to change. When that happened, I knew had nowhere to go but up.

For most of my life, I had a love-hate relationship with food. How I loved the comfort that food gave me, but oh, how bad I felt (and was made to feel by others) as a result of stuffing my mouth nonstop. Consequently, I suffered both mentally and physically.

I berated myself for my inability to control my eating for decades and wished the most horrible things upon myself. I knew the power that food had over me, and I wanted nothing more than to control it and myself, but I simply couldn't.

I wanted to just stop eating and go cold turkey. To be successful in other programs, such as those that help you stop smoking or drinking, you must completely omit things from your life, like cigarettes or alcohol. This is doable because neither is life-sustaining. However, taking this approach for losing weight isn't realistic because completely omitting food from your life is not an option. You need the nourishment that food offers.

I can remember getting a cold as a kid and not really being able to taste anything. I longingly said to my mom while slurping a mouthful of salty, yummy, canned chicken noodle soup, "I wish my taste buds would stop working like this all the time."

She looked at me, her eyebrows furrowed with puzzlement. "Why?"

"So that I wouldn't like eating."

Many of us have had similar experiences where we wished we would just stop putting so much exhausting energy into food and food choices. We go through that damned-if-you-do-and-damned-if-you-don't nightmare, analyzing every bite before, during, and after we've devoured it. Whether it's a crunchy carrot or a slice of carrot cake, it doesn't matter; we'll always judge our choices. But if we make a conscious decision to eat and enjoy the cake, we'll *still* scold ourselves and feel bad.

You know the drill. You justify that tiny morsel of cake or cookie or whatever and say you're going to love every morsel. What happens after you eat it, though? You don't allow yourself to revel in what you've eaten. Instead, old feelings of shame and guilt kick in, and your brain goes on a rampage as it batters your self-esteem in the process. The subconscious takes over, *even though you just made a rational decision to enjoy the cake or cookie.*

What's worse is that for many of us, it's not a simple word or two of scolding; it's a deep, long-winded message that constantly tells you that you have no willpower, that you can't control yourself, and well, that you're basically a loser. The toxic combination of guilt and shame often leads people down a slippery slope from which it's really hard to escape. Uncontrolled, it can create some really bad habits and as in my case, lead to other self-destructive behaviors.

First and foremost, it's important to note that guilt and shame are *not* the same things. If broken down into the simplest form, shame is the belief that you are not enough, not lovable, and not worthy because you're bad to the core. For example, "I'm an undeserving, bad person and worthless because I ate that piece of cake."

Guilt, on the other hand, is simply the feeling you get when you've *done something bad.* "Man, I shouldn't have had that second piece of pizza." It doesn't judge you as a person; it simply judges your actions. Guilt is often productive, and it helps to keep us in check. Shame, however, is nothing but destructive. More importantly, it's *wrong.*

When it came to food, boy, I felt both shame and guilt, which were what led me to do some really unhealthy, dangerous things while growing up. Let me tell you, though, when it came to experiencing those emotions, good ole Catholic mothers had *nothing* on me. I served up and generously dolloped an enormous amount of guilt *and* shame upon myself on a daily basis.

Everything I ate from a piece of fruit to a granola bar and beyond transcended from the simple nourishment that it was intended to be to a debate and analysis of giant proportions.

"How many points does it have on the program? Is it even allowed? Does it have too many carbs? Is it too high in fat? What's the fiber content? How many grams of sugar?" On and on and on it went until I was so damned hungry I just ate it and suffered the self-assault afterwards.

No doubt a deep-seated hunger dwelt within me, something that truly needed to be fed emotionally and physically. No matter what I ate, it just didn't satisfy, so I kept eating. I constantly looked for the next fix, trying to fill the void and trying to heal. I only wound up feeling numb.

I had no idea at the time why I had such a physical, insatiable appetite, why my hunger continued to remain in the forefront of my mind, and why I continually stuffed food in my mouth. The eat-and-beat cycle became a part of my everyday life at a very early age, and the harsh shame I felt from submitting to my hunger seemed to be reinforced everywhere.

The results of my incessant food consumption started to show. All of those extra empty calories I ate to anesthetize my pain started to catch up with me in a very big way on several different levels. I wasn't just a tall adolescent anymore; now I was also fat.

Other kids began to pick on me at school because of my height and my weight. I got bullied at the bus stop, which humiliated me. I felt like an outcast, and I felt like the fatso my Auntie had called me years ago.

With no friends who could relate and with parents who told me to simply ignore my peers, I had nowhere to turn. No one understood. I started to really *feel* the difference in how I was treated, not only in the outside world but at home as well.

My mom was particularly concerned and unhappy about my weight. As an adult I can now see that her intentions were pure and that she didn't want to see me suffer. As a vulnerable child, however, her help and desire for me to lose weight came across like punishment. I felt even more "less than." I felt as if she didn't love me because I was fat. I felt that because I wasn't thin, I wasn't a good-enough kid. I felt I needed to try harder and harder to be better so that I could make her happy and get attention. It was a shame tsunami.

When I was around eleven years old, my mother started putting me on all of the different diets. With them came conflicting messages that made no sense. I remember how virtually every morning my mom took two over-the-counter diet pills from the shiny yellow box, one for her and one for me. She always seemed to be on a diet too, but I never remember her being anything even close to overweight.

I obediently popped the pill along with my Flintstones chewable vitamin. Breakfast and the onslaught of food then followed. After all, mom had said that breakfast was the most important meal of the day, and we couldn't leave the house without eating it.

Home became a prison where I was under twenty-four-hour watch. My mom monitored and scrutinized everything I ate. No matter what the food was, I got "the look" with every morsel I put on my plate. I wasn't allowed to eat dessert. Butter on my potato was forbidden. Water or skim milk was the only beverage I could drink.

I could no longer find joy in food whatsoever. While the rest of my family enjoyed whatever they wanted, I sat at the table with my plate in front of me and felt nothing but anger and shame.

Since I was the only one in my family who was under guard, I was on my own with no support or encouragement, only scrutiny. This was difficult for me, especially since bad foods were not eliminated from our house, and oh, what a bounty of things there were. However, my parents simply ordered me not to eat them.

Furthermore, my father had his own cupboard with cookies and chips that my brother and I were not allowed to touch. Nothing screams "you're bad" like being forbidden from doing, well, anything.

Although both my parents worked, we never missed a meal. When my dad returned home at the end of the day, we stuck with a routine, which always included dinner, a family-must in my house. Sometimes mom cooked; sometimes dad cooked. Regardless, a plentiful amount of food was always on the table during dinnertime.

When the eighties arrived, many more women entered the workforce. Consequently, the need for fast, prepared foods were in demand, so the grocery stores erupted with new prepared meal choices and quick and easy dishes to try.

My mom was part of that workforce with a full-time job as a labor-and-delivery nurse at the local hospital. She worked a swing-shift schedule with long and crazy hours. Even so, one thing was certain: something would be on the table for dinner.

Our evening meals consisted of fast food and boxed culinary delights like frozen Salisbury steaks smothered in gravy, LaChoy chow mein right out of the can, tuna noodle casseroles glistening in mushroom soup, fried SPAM burgers, crispy, golden Banquet fried chicken served with crispy tater tots straight from the oven, and other mouthwatering delicious delights. I learned how to operate the oven early on, but the unsupervised stovetop was strictly off limits.

The day dad came home with the new microwave, you would have thought Jesus himself had walked in the door with a box. We all stood around the counter as dad plugged it in the wall, set the clock, opened the microwave door, and put a cup of water inside. Behold the power and the glory of two minutes to boiling. Cooking with this new contraption was fun, it was safe, and in many ways, it opened the door to my culinary experimentation. It also gave me new poison for my addiction.

We wanted to microwave everything. Quite frankly, I marvel as to how that microwave actually survived in our house. My brother, five years my junior, microwaved everything he could put his hands on, most of which should have never been in a microwave whatsoever, such as the cordless phone. (Yes, Mom, if you're reading this book, that's what *really* happened to our phone.)

Oh, how our afterschool snacks took on a whole new light. We raced home to see who could come up with the best concoctions in the microwave. No more grab-and-go snacks for us. No sir! Who wanted to eat an apple or veggies when you could have salty, slippery, hot, and yummy pizza pockets or— *wait for it*—a cup full of squiggly, delicious ramen noodles in just a minute?

Let's not forget the wonder food of my youth: Velveeta cheese. The thought of that yellow box stuffed full of cool, soft, and velvety decadence stimulated my salivary glands like nothing else. I could have eaten a whole box myself (and probably did). It was a snack made in heaven that no one could resist.

Afterschool snacks were the best. My parents weren't home at that time to watch what I ate, so any food I secretly consumed got blamed on my brother. My scheme was all very convenient and worked beautifully to hide my secret eating

The new trends in food were all about making it easy, inexpensive, tasty, and the foods with their high fat, salt, and flavor content were ridiculously addictive. The surge in popularity meant food manufacturers kept churning out delicacies. We, along with many of my peers, became easily obsessed in a new world of choices.

I could go on and on, but chances are you get exactly where I'm coming from if you're reading this book. In fact, you probably have a few of your own favorites foods that cause you to cringe as you look back on them now while at the same time, you may also be secretly craving them. We've all been there (and still are).

Mom did make many homemade meals as well, and we were blessed with fresh fruits and vegetables galore. We had a couple of acres of farmland where we grew corn on the cob, green beans, peppers, strawberries, blueberries, raspberries, and so much more. My first job was "wo-manning" the farm stand at the end of our driveway. People drove for miles for our veggies, especially the corn. I garnered a lot from the experience, and it led me to become an entrepreneur but certainly not a farmer. While my parents have thumbs so green they need to be mowed, I killed houseplants. Who knew they needed water?

My parents both worked very hard in the garden and at their jobs to make ends meet. We were never a wealthy family by any stretch. My dad grew up on a farm where food was grown and slaughtered, and nothing went to waste.

My mom grew up poor, and her father had died when she was nine and didn't leave much for his family. She was often hungry as a child. She told me years later that her goal in life was to make sure her children were never hungry, and her deepest desire was to provide plenty for her family. As a result, she felt rejected and like a failure if we appeared disinterested in eating what she had prepared.

Within my family, I could easily see how the fear and loathing of wasting food was passed down from generation to generation. Food cost a lot of money. Money was precious, therefore so was food. Showing appreciation for the person who also prepared the food was an important part of that value equation. To reject the food was to devalue both the person who worked to acquire it and the person who prepared it. In a way, food took on a currency all its own.

The old messages in her head about throwing things away, food going to waste, and her own shame blindsided her from seeing how her feelings about food affected me mentally and physically.

As a working woman, I can appreciate the effort that goes into getting a meal on the table. However, food is not love when it is served in excess and with our own agenda.

I felt as though my parents were oblivious to the mixed messages they sent, though. Both sternly believed in the "Clean-Plate Club." You were required to eat what was provided and finish your meal. It's just what you did, no questions asked, and you could *not* leave the table until you were done. So on one hand, I was required to eat everything on my plate, but on the other hand they wanted me to lose weight. Logically I'm sure they knew that in order for me to lose weight, they needed to feed me less.

I found myself in a lose-lose situation, a hopeless spiral from which I couldn't break free. My parent's constant critique, both of the food on my plate and of the numbers on the scale was agonizing. I was literally damned if I did and damned if I didn't.

You've probably experienced something similar. Someone in your life who *just wants the best for you* comments on your food choices and questions your motives. As adults hearing these messages, we recognize that for the most part the scrutiny comes from a place of good intention. People want what is best for us and want us to be happy, but emotionally it causes us to feel less than and not good enough. As children receiving these messages, the words are more than damaging.

Deep down we want what's best for us. We want health, good eating habits, and to be in our best bodies. However, this often feels elusive. So rather than believe that we can reach our goals, we listen to what others say and find comfort in staying small and in believing we can't meet our goals no matter how hard we try. We stay satisfied in feeling less than. We make an agreement with ourselves that we will never be successful. Simply giving up and feeling miserable is far easier than facing reality and admitting we just don't know what to do. I know. I spent way too many years there. I'm happy to report that there is a way out.

When it comes down to it, we need to take our personal power back and *stop* caring so much about what other people think. Don't we beat ourselves up enough? Do we *really* need someone else watching out for us? The answer is no, and when it happens to you, you need to ignore it and tell the other person to mind his or her own business. Period. Remember, you're living life by your rules and no one else's.

As a kid, I didn't have that luxury or ability to stick up for myself. As parents, we need to be very careful about saying harmful words or passing on our bad beliefs when it comes to our children and other young people in our lives. We have the ability to shame with our words and with our actions in ways that we may perceive to be harmless.

One of my most painful memories comes from one evening when I was around thirteen. My dad liked to treat my brother and me, and so he took us to the local ice cream shop for cones. My younger brother and I stood at the counter, gleefully reading down the flavor choices out loud and trying hard to make a decision. Halfway through the list, my dad looked at me with a furrowed brow and arms crossed and said, "Nothing but sherbet for you."

Whether or not he thought that was the best low-calorie option for me, or whether he was under strict instruction from my mom, I'll never know. The outcome was the same either way. I was shamed and mortified that I was a bad girl, that my "treat" came with conditions, and that I couldn't have what I wanted.

When my time came to order, I looked at my dad pleadingly. In return, he gave me the wide-eyed "you-better-listen" look. I ordered my stupid rainbow sherbet cone and sat on the stoop, not enjoying a single lick but eating it all anyway. To this day, I can't walk into that chain of stores and see the ice-cream flavor board without remembering that trip decades ago. Needless to say, I also abhor sherbet.

What's ironic to me now is that we've become much more nutritionally aware. Since then we've learned that sherbet actually contains *more* sugar calories than ice cream, but I digress. In his fatherly wisdom, my dad believed he had helped me.

It is so important for all of us to remember that unsolicited advice, no matter how well-intended, is still criticism. We all need to pay careful attention to how we use our words, especially with those we claim to love.

The constant watching, berating, and most of all, my lack of success in losing any weight pissed me off royally, but I could do very little about any of them. I continued to feel helpless, hopeless, and worthless. In defiance and frustration, I ate even more in an attempt to comfort myself.

In no time, my teenage shame turned into teenage anger and rebellion. I started to get really mad and formed some really destructive behaviors.

My anger toward my parents started with the ever-repeating "eat this, not that" evening-dinner argument that we engaged in almost nightly. No matter what I said, no one listened to me or allowed me to choose what I wanted to eat and how much. I steamed inside, not being able to simply be heard. Eventually I learned to just keep quiet and eat my portion.

When the meals were over, I was required to stay behind to help clean up the kitchen. Right afterwards, I excused myself and promptly went to the bathroom where I shoved my fingers down my throat and threw up everything I ate.

Nothing felt better than to purge myself of all the food I had eaten. Voiding the poison from my system, letting go of what others had seemingly forced me to consume, and taking control of myself, was such a relief. As destructive as it was, as physically horrible as it felt, it served its purpose.

While I didn't purge often, I used the action as a way to gain control whenever I felt out of control. When I had overeaten or when I felt horrible about myself after a binge, I crammed my fingers down my throat as a coping mechanism to feel powerful.

My parents knew I made myself vomit and gave me a stern talking to. Even that conversation wasn't compassionate. Instead what I received was a lecture from my father who simply said, "You're a bad girl. Stop doing that."

My insatiable hunger for comfort, unconditional love, and acceptance grew larger and larger along with my waistline. As a teen I cried out for attention, and still no one listened. No one knew about the excruciating pain I felt, of my struggle, and of my internal turmoil. I'm not even sure I could have put words to it at that age.

In frustration, I started shoplifting little items from the drugstore for attention. Most of the time I stole something to make me feel pretty, like makeup. Other times I stole candy.

One day at the local mall during a Christmas shopping trip with my father and my brother, I got busted. I remember sitting at the officer's desk in the police station and saying, "I'm happy you caught me." And I was. Finally, I'd get some attention. I was no longer the *good girl*. At last someone would finally notice me. Although my shoplifting ended that day, nothing else did in my family.

I didn't know what to do, and no one was happy with me. I got heavier, and I was lonely and scared, which only made me want to eat more and more. So I started seriously hiding food and what I ate.

Of course I fooled no one but myself. I conveniently blamed my brother again when the containers of whipped cream and ice cream unexpectedly wound up empty.

When I was away from home, the sky was the limit. Anywhere there was food, I gave myself carte blanche to eat whatever I wanted because no one watched over me, and no one seemed to care.

I stole food while I babysat, raiding the cupboards for anything that looked good and then purging afterwards. I *really* hated myself for that one. I experienced the guilt, not only from throwing up but from literally "stealing" from people who entrusted me to care for their kids and their home. It was horrible.

Christine, my very best friend in high school, was my biggest advocate. (In fact, we remain BFFs to this day). Although a little overweight herself, she never experienced the same weight issues I did, and she was sympathetic to my situation.

Her mom (mom number-two in those days) was an amazing, and I mean an amazing baker. She kept her house stocked with goodies, and I simply *loved* going over there. She always had something in the oven, and buckets of frosting were at our disposal. Her butterscotch oatmeal cookies were the bomb, and I could eat them by the dozens...and did.

I'll never forget the shame and embarrassment I felt one summer when I went on a week-long camping trip with Chris' family. Of course, mom number-two had made my favorite cookies, and she kept them in a box in the camper. Chris and I had our own tent, yet somehow several times a day, I found myself alone in the camper sneaking cookies.

Later in the week, Chris' dad went to get some cookies for himself and discovered the box was pretty much empty. He angrily went to Chris' mom wanting to know what happened to them.

She simply replied, "Stacey ate them all."

No one ever knew I overheard this exchange. I was consciously aware that I had been going into the camper for cookies, yet I was in denial. Obviously just about everyone around knew I was the culprit, and hearing that declaration out loud simply devastated me.

The shame of sneaking food and hiding what I ate, of binging and purging and not knowing what else to do, of disappointing my parents for not cleaning my plate, and yet *still* being fat, well, it got to be too much.

Not knowing what else to do, I simply gave up. I stopped fighting the battle against food and gave into my cravings without a care in the world.

3
FITTING IN

"You are here not to shrink down to less,
but to blossom into more of who you really are."
—Oprah Winfrey

Someone recently asked me if I had been overweight in high school. I honestly needed to stop and think because I didn't know the *real* answer. I can't recall whether or not I was actually obese or if by comparison I was just that much larger than my friends. I can't recall looking at myself in mirrors, and I don't know if that's because I consciously avoided them as much as I could.

If not for photos, I'm not sure I could remember just what my body looked like. I only recall the strong emotions associated with how I felt—huge. In looking back at those photos now, I see that in actuality, from the young age of ten or eleven when I hit puberty, I already had the body of a woman, not a teenager, and I was chunky but by no means obese. However at the time, there was no telling myself that I was anything other than very large. I only knew how I *felt*, and that was *fat*, and that feeling seemed to be reinforced everywhere I went.

Whether I was at school or at home, I was always attuned to what I *thought* other people said about me. No matter if they paid me a compliment directly or if I saw them looking at me and whispering, I always assumed that what they said was bad even if it wasn't.

I reinforced this notion by creating entire stories in my mind about their comments and conversations. In truth, I had *no idea* what they were really talking about or if they were even talking about me. However, I considered my stories to be the truth.

The fact of the matter was, I truly believed that I was huge and that everyone else thought less of me and made fun of me for my size. Nothing anyone could say to me would cause me think otherwise.

To be fair, I really was taller and curvier than the average kid. By age thirteen, I was five foot eight and wore a double d bra. To say I didn't know what to do with my body was the understatement of the century. I just never fit in anywhere. I was happy for the scant few friends I had and mistrusted everyone else around me.

Teenage years were awkward enough but add in the anomaly of my size, and the overall awkwardness of this era just compounded every effort I made to blend in. As a girl, we all know how much emphasis is placed on appearance, wearing the right clothes, and conforming to the norms. I had absolutely tanked in this department, literally. I could never find clothes to fit me. In those days the fashion choices for a girl who could only wear women's sizes were in very short supply, and that's only if any supply existed at all.

You'd think that having a great seamstress as a mother was a fabulous benefit, especially since she ran a little fabric store out of our basement, and it was. I had the greatest book bags, purses, and pillows. Although my bedroom curtains were gorgeous, my wardrobe was anything but.

Mom's idea of fashion vastly differed from my own. She made what she thought were amazing outfits but ones I absolutely despised. Many mornings ended in fights, arguments, and yelling matches. I wore what she wanted and then changed at school, or I simply resorted to my tried-and-true outfits: oversized jeans and baggy men's shirts and sweatshirts. They were big, comfy, and hid my chest, and they were oh-so chic...not. But what's a girl to do?

By high school, I had picked up enough seamstress skills to begin creating my own wardrobe. I became quite pleased and proud of my creations. They were a great solution to an awkward problem, but I still never felt like I was enough. All of the other girls wore designer jeans, such as Calvin Klein, Jordache, or Gloria Vanderbilt, with beautiful, frilly feminine tops by Gunne Sax. I wore whatever I could get my hands on and what fit.

I was determined not to allow the fashion goddesses in the magazines or in my school get the upper hand. Nope, not me. They may have said, "You'll never fit in" but I said, "Watch me win."

I was convinced that one way or the other, I could have the wardrobe (and therefore the in-crowd acceptance) that those other girls had. Nothing would stop me. My determination to be part of the "in crowd" was fierce.

In fact to this day, one of my mom's favorite sayings about me is *if you want something done, tell Stacey not to do it.*

As a tenth-grader rebelling and wanting to desperately fit in, I worked and saved the money I had earned for months from a babysitting job so that I could buy my very own designer jeans. My mom drove me to the mall, and in I hurried to the hallowed ground of *Bay Street*, the "it" destination for denim. Much like my trip to the shoe store years before, I walked in and became dazzled.

This shopping trip turned out to be very different, though. No longer was I an innocent girl with wide-eyed wonder looking at all of the possibilities, colors, shapes, and styles in front of me. The former joy that had sparked my imagination as to who I could be—a powerful, strong, feminine woman like Wonder Woman or one of Charlie's Angels—had vanished. All I wanted now was the jeans, *the* key to fitting in, to getting accepted, to becoming part of the crowd. I didn't *want* those jeans; I *needed* them.

I was a girl on a mission as I feverishly went through the abundant selection and reviewed pair after pair. After what seemed like an hour, I walked out absolutely dejected. I had gone through every pair they had, yet I couldn't find any that worked for me. The largest pairs fit (if I sucked it in, wiggled a bit to zip them up, and didn't sit down while wearing them), but the standard lengths were far too short. They looked ridiculous.

Now don't think for one minute that I didn't stand there staring at the jeans in the dressing room mirror convincing myself that they *could* work *if* I wore them with the right socks or right shoes, etc. I considered every possibility. Having no other choice, I simply gave up. I would have given anything to have walked out of that store with some jeans, any jeans. It was simply not to be. Once again I was a failure, even with buying a stupid pair of jeans.

My designer-jean dream had come crashing down. My mom offered to take me to the department store for another pair of regular jeans, but I was despondent. I thought her completely insensitive for not understanding my plight. No other jeans would do. For me at that time, resorting back to my wardrobe status quo wasn't the solution. I wanted to break out and place myself into the jeans that would allow me to fit in.

This unsuccessful shopping trip devastated me. I had worked hard. I had saved, and I had given it my all. I dared to reach for success. I did *everything right*. I tried to reach for my dreams and failed. Once again the world simply reinforced that I was a freak of nature, leaving me feeling more displaced than ever, all because of a pair of jeans.

With the rapid onset of puberty and all of the changes I started going through, my body quickly became the enemy. I felt like a doll with rubber arms and legs being pulled and pushed in all physical directions. My boobs popped out, and my hips stretched far and wide. My head got pulled toward the ceiling, and my arms no longer fit inside my shirts. I had no control over any of it.

This time period became an uncomfortable one all the way around. Physically I experienced such bad growing pains in my legs that they kept me up at night tossing and turning and crying in discomfort. Mentally the anguish built. Spiritually, well, my mom dragged us to church, but at that age I found the whole thing rather hypocritical. In essence, mentally, physically, and spiritually, I had nothing to hold onto, nothing for comfort. My support structure was nil. I had nowhere to turn except back to the good old comfort of food, so I kept right on eating.

Sideshow Stacey

Because of my size and *good-girl* mannered rules, many thought I was much older than my tender years. I got a lot of attention for many different reasons, and none of them seemed positive from my perspective. My parents appeared to get a kick out of telling anyone who commented on my height or size that I was "only this old" instead of the many years older that person assumed I was.

I understand now that this was a matter of pride for them, but as a kid I felt more like a sideshow. I started getting attention from boys as well. Looking like I did with my well-developed body, I suppose it was only natural, but this type of attention freaked out my mom. Of course it freaked me out too because I wasn't prepared for the kind of interest they showed me. Why would anyone (especially a boy) notice *me*? I had nothing to offer. Plus in my mind's eye, I was fat. Who could possibly be interested in me? I was convinced that any attention I received was nothing but a joke and that someone was out to get me or make fun of me.

My mom's discomfort over my blossoming body came from a completely different angle. I wasn't exactly a planned pregnancy, which was no secret in my family. My mom and dad (who are still together) got pregnant with me at an unexpectedly early age. So you can understand why my mom got very, very scared when she saw the attention I was receiving from young men. She made it her job to do everything she could to keep me "safe."

Through her good intentions, I was pretty much "desexualized" and given very mixed messages about what it meant to be a woman at an early age. On one hand, she encouraged me to be like the other girls so that I could fit in, but on the other hand and in many ways, she didn't actually allow me to be a girl and tried her best to hide my developing body.

My mom didn't sit me down one day with a list of rules. They started creeping in slowly as I began to model after my peers and then attempted to copy some of their behaviors. I saw actresses on TV who influenced how I wanted to wear my hair and makeup. I wanted to explore things that made a girl a girl and further pursue the idea of fitting in with my peers. These were simple things I could apply that had nothing to do with wardrobe and my size.

When I sought permission from my mom (remember that I was "the good girl"), she flat-out denied my requests to explore my personal style. My hair could not be changed. It had to stay short. My earrings had to be small and not gaudy. I was not allowed to wear makeup until I was older.

No wonder my previously mentioned petty-theft activities included makeup. This was no coincidence. Eye shadow and lipstick fit so easily into a pocket, both for sneaking out of the store and sneaking into school. Of course let's not forget how easily they could be applied on the bus long before anyone saw me arrive at school and then wiped off before I got home.

All things about my appearance became more and more important, yet at every turn, I felt like I just couldn't win when it came to fashion and keeping up with how my friends looked. My mom kept my thick, curly, unruly hair cropped short. Remember the Dorothy Hamill cut? Yeah, I rocked that. I wanted long hair so much, but my mom simply said, "No."

It didn't stop there. My mom banned everything but sneakers and flats from my feet, and you know my love of shoes. As mentioned before, my wardrobe was lackluster. In addition to not finding much that fit, my mom placed restrictions on what I could wear. Anything lower cut was forbidden. Anything clingy was a no-go. Furthermore, I was *not* allowed to wear anything black because she said, "Only whores wear black." The whole battle with her was frustrating, humiliating, and just plain horrible.

At the local thrift store I found a great book on how to be a stylish larger woman. The title and author's name are long gone from my brain, but the image of the beautiful brunette on the cover, her beaming smile, lively eyes, and great style were inspirational and unforgettable. She looked so happy, so stylish, and so put together, even with her larger-than-normal size. The fact that she had been picked for the cover encouraged me. I was more than impressed and couldn't wait to dive into reading how I could be the same.

My mom came home and saw me reading the book. The look she gave me at the sight of the cover was of pure disgust. I felt such shame, such rejection from her glare that I went to my room, put the book under my bed, and cried. A week later when I went to read the book again, it was gone. I felt so alone.

The shame, guilt, anger, and frustration that arose from the lack of correct guidance and support were excruciating. All I wanted was her understanding and empathy. Instead I got rules and the constant message that I did nothing but disappoint her and my father. Worse was the rationale or reasons behind her rules that were never explained or discussed. She simply said, "Because I said so."

Even though I now truly believe her intentions were good, nothing makes a kid want to rebel more than the four words "Because I said so." I was no different. They only fueled my anger. While they would provide guidance for me as an adult and with parenting my own daughter later on, hearing them at the time was incredibly awkward and painful. Again, words hurt.

My dad avoided all interaction with this kind of "girly" stuff altogether. He deferred to my mom and got angry if I went to him looking for support. When I did, I was called defiant, accused of trying to play one parent against the other, and that what my mom said goes.

In truth, I wasn't trying to play anyone. I was just looking for someone, anyone who would cut me a break and who would understand and validate what I felt. I know my mom only wanted the best for me, and her reactions to my changing body simply came from panic and fear, but I wanted to scream. I only wish that the messages she tried to convey could have been channeled in a positive, uplifting way rather than becoming a source of shame that would haunt me well into my later years.

Like a broken record, the words *I'm horrible, I'm a disappointment,* and *I'm huge* kept playing in my head. I looked *nothing like* the girls in the *Teen* and *Seventeen* magazines. Those girls I went to school with were mostly average size and seemed to be so happy.

I fantasized about moving to California, so that while there I'd feel *so bad* when I looked at all of the other beautiful women, I'd have no choice but to lose weight. I spent countless hours fantasizing about scenarios like this, ones that would somehow allow me to do what I couldn't seem to do on my own.

I was sized like an adult but not welcomed in their circles either. All of my mom's friends seemed to empathize pitifully, not with *me* and my plight, but with my mom and what she had to go through *with me.* Of course hearing this made me feel even worse.

I didn't come to understand until later that they empathized because they saw the beautiful, full-breasted, tall, and *seemingly* confident young woman I was becoming. Of course my extreme metamorphosis would be a challenge for my mom (or any mom) to handle. When I heard their comments, though, all that registered in my mind was, "Oh, you poor mother. Your daughter is hideous."

I might have seemed confident on the outside, but inside I was anything but. In addition to being larger than my peers and feeling like I didn't fit in, I didn't have any girlfriends who I could talk with about fashion or makeup or boyfriends,

My shame went deep. I hated my height. I hated my boobs. I hated my mom. I hated my dad. I hated myself. I just wanted to hide.

Wanting to have some friends, I found myself hanging with the boys. The guys who were my age or even a few years older had been safe; they didn't seem to judge or care. They didn't talk about the latest fashion or the latest gossip. They just "were."

Even though boys seemed less competitive than the girls, I still mistrusted them. My lack of positive experiences around them made me wary. While I was okay with being their friend, I definitely felt very body conscious around them. One minute I'd feel fine talking about music or sports, but the next I'd feel insecure and uncomfortable as they glanced at my chest.

One story in particular still makes me cringe. We had always spent a summer week at the Jersey Shore. Whether we hung out on the beach, at the pool, or you name it, we were out there soaking up the sun and the fun.

On a beautiful, sunny day, I had been lounging poolside reading and loving every minute of it. Music played in the background, a diet soda cooled my hand, and my little brother was nowhere to be found. All in all, life was good.

Two "older" guys walked by me. They were probably in their late teens or early twenties. After passing I heard one say rather loudly to the other, "Holy s**t! Did you see the size of the tits on that chick?"

My good mood turned sour instantly. I'm sure the guy meant his comment as sheer fascination in a good way, but in my shame state, all I heard was, "She's fat, ugly, and hideous with *huge* boobs!" The bad-girl cassette tape started playing again in my brain and wouldn't stop.

I felt crushed. I went back to the hotel room and stayed there for the remainder of the day, crying and feeling dejected. I again felt so ashamed, and I couldn't tell anyone why.

During my junior year of high school, things started to change. I began to accept my evolving body for the better as my hormonally lagging girlfriends started to catch up. We began to "even out," so to say, finding ourselves all in a confusing teenage pool of uncertainty. We found some unity in our collective misery.

The best thing to happen that year was a boyfriend. Yes, hanging out with the guys led to an amazing friend, confidant, and partner in crime with whom I had been spending a lot of time.

Two years younger than me, he was my *everything*, or so I thought. We were equally tall and stood eye to eye. I believed that his big, broad shoulders could protect me from harm and keep me safe. We became inseparable, and I truly believed I could *not* live without him.

With him, I had found someone in whom I could confide my deepest secrets. I had someone who gave me unconditional love and gifts and made me feel like I was *special*. When I was with him, he removed any questions I had about my being pretty. He lavished me with attention, and I reciprocated. I was head over heels in love.

A bit of a misfit himself, he accepted me for who I was, weight and all. Yet no matter how much attention he paid me, how much he showed me he loved me, or how much he *told* me he loved me, nothing he did ever allowed me to feel "enough."

Even with the unconditional love and acceptance from another person, I still suffered a horrible void. I compared myself again to all of the role models I had around me, on television, in magazines, and of course to the girls at school, and I failed. I continued to ask myself how this amazing, handsome man could be with *me* when I was such a miserable failure. I thought I surely didn't deserve him. In spite of my insecurities, he stayed by my side.

At that tender age (hell, at just about *any age)*, we can't help but take the social cues that are given around us about what's acceptable and what's not, compare and contrast ourselves to our peers in a very critical way, and then experience detrimental results. As an adult, I have since reflected back with some high school friends about the awkwardness we *all* felt. I discovered that apparently many, if not most of us, never felt as though we were enough when it came to our bodies.

We need to learn to bridge the gap between self-acceptance and perceived reality. It's time to put all the airbrushing and retouching to rest, practice self-love, and stop our self-loathing. We need to do this not only for our own sanity, but for the health and well-being of our daughters (and sons) and for the greater good of the world. We must stop beating ourselves up and understand that we are physically perfect just as we are.

As teens and young adults, we are at our most impressionable. The thoughts, messages, and things we tell ourselves (and those that others tell us) can have a positive or negative impact on us for the remainder of our life.

However, even with what I call bad programming, we can still prosper. It just takes determination and time.

4

THE DEBUTANTE

"Let go of certainty. The opposite isn't uncertainty.
It's openness, curiosity and a willingness
to embrace paradox,
rather than choose up sides.
The ultimate challenge is to accept ourselves
exactly as we are,
but never stop trying to learn and grow."
—Tony Schwartz

The summer after my senior year of high school found me with mixed emotions.

I had been accepted to an amazing college about two hours away from home, and I excitedly looked forward to leaving behind the confines of family. As an avid adventure seeker and risk taker, I was eager to begin and explore a whole new chapter in my life.

On the other hand, I was in love. My boyfriend and I had done everything together, and we had been virtually inseparable every day since we had met almost two years earlier. I had no idea how I would live without him. How I would function? How I would survive?

We agreed to write. He promised to call me when he could and come to visit on the weekends. For the time being, this plan seemed doable.

So on that fateful August day that we both knew would arrive, I packed my parents' car, hopped in, and left my boyfriend to go to college. I was only two hours away and still in the state of New York, but you would have thought I had been exiled to Alaska. I was devastated.

I was assigned to a huge coed dorm and in a room with two other girls who were complete strangers. Up until then, I had never shared a room with anyone. I found myself feeling quite alone. With not knowing anyone and little-to-no contact with my family or my guy, I felt completely lost.

When I think about dorm life back then, I can't help but smile at the craziness. We only had one pay phone for the entire floor, and we always had to wait to call out unless you were up at two a.m. Virtually no one could call in to leave messages for us either. The inability to communicate to the outside world was torturous because the most important thing in my life was two hours away.

Every day I ran to my mailbox and was frequently greeted with a card, a letter, or even flowers on special occasions like Valentine's Day. I went home on weekends, or he came to visit me, and we always took advantage of a few vacation breaks here and there.

We made it through that first year, but it wasn't easy. I missed him horribly. I often found myself calling him incessantly or writing letters or wanting to contact him just to hear him tell me I would be all right, that I was all right, and that we would survive. I realize now how much I relied on his validation, his acceptance, and his words to give me the sense of self-worth I needed on a daily basis. I had become classically co-dependent.

The following May I happily packed up all of my belongings at school and headed home, looking forward to a summer of fun, excitement, and adventure. I couldn't wait to have all the time in the world with my guy and to be back in his arms.

However, our reunion came across as disappointing. Although I was so excited to see him and feverishly talked about plans for the summer, I could tell something was wrong with him. He seemed distant and not as affectionate.

Not long afterward and without much explanation, he dumped me by sending me a note saying he didn't want to be together anymore and that we were done. And that was that.

Just as I had fallen head over heels in love with this boy, I fell even harder at the rejection. I discovered that another girl had taken my place and that I was no longer needed.

To this very day I remember the moment I found out about "her." I had been walking downtown with a few of my girlfriends, and he drove by with her in the car for all to witness. They were laughing, playing music, and having a great time. I simply couldn't believe what I saw.

My heart pounded. My vision blurred. I wanted to throw up. I felt a hot, burning sensation rise throughout my whole body. Little did I know at the time, but actual sensations of shame often take on a physical form in this way, and I experienced them to the max.

My world had just crumbled. I felt so unwanted, so unloved, so valueless. How could I have been replaced?

Thus began my grieving process as I continued to take the breakup hard and all very personally. What did I have to live for? What did she have that I didn't have? I just kept asking myself what I had done wrong.

I unleashed my anger by calling him every bad name in the book to his face. I called all of his friends. I wrote and delivered nasty letters. I called up his favorite publications pretending to be him and requested that his magazine subscriptions be canceled. I did everything I could to make him feel the pain I felt. Little could I have known at the time, but my anger and frustration had nothing to do with him and had everything to do with me.

I think I cried for a month straight. I couldn't function, and I spiraled into a deep depression. But boy, could I eat. I've heard how some people totally lose their appetite during a breakup, but not me. I went the other direction, and I mean hard. I didn't want to talk to anyone. I didn't want to see any of my friends. I just wanted to be consoled through stuffing my mouth.

That summer, I worked as a waitress at the local barbeque joint. I had easy access to the best comfort food around, and I relished every morsel of the job's benefits in excess.

The trip back to school that fall was very different than the previous year. This time I counted the days until the start of the semester and couldn't wait to run away from home and away from the hurt. I just wanted to hide. After all, disappearing into the oblivion of campus life would make everything better. I could focus on school and totally forget about home.

When I got back to school, I threw myself into campus life. As a sophomore I moved to an on-campus townhome with nine other girls. We no longer had to contend with floors of people. We were our own little family.

While I had a decent set of acquaintances at school, I still experienced the ongoing feelings of not fitting in, and this time with a larger school population. I assumed the role of a quiet outcast. I went to parties; I had friends; and on the outside I made all appear well, but on the inside, I still struggled and still tried to find my way. I had no sense of belonging unless I was out partying.

Of course nothing seemed to really matter when you were drunk. I went out with my housemates to the local bars and found myself sitting alone nursing a drink while they flirted or danced. When others joined me, I allowed myself to go with the flow, laughing and happily blending into the conversation. These were some of the few times when I felt accepted and *at home*.

Reflecting back now, I can see that I felt this way because the alcohol allowed me to let down my guard. I was always a happy drunk. In my inebriated state, I could be my true self and feel like no one was out to hurt me.

Outside the bar atmosphere, I started drinking a lot more than I should have. I hung out with different groups and tried to find somewhere, anywhere I could be comfortable. Searching for more than just casual groups and conversation, longing for that sense of validation and self-worth, and needing to recoup what I had felt with my boyfriend, I discovered I was boy crazy. I wanted so much to again experience those feelings of safety, security, and love. I wanted to feel beautiful and adored and purposeful.

I thought a guy was the answer to all my problems. Because of my youthfulness and immaturity, I was convinced that the only way to satisfy those desires would be through someone else. I needed another person to give it to me. I needed a man. How I expected to "find" one, I had no idea. Desperate, disheveled, fat, and really out of shape, I didn't exactly present my best self.

My weight had blossomed at that time to well over two hundred pounds. College food, drinking, late-night snacks, and other indiscriminate eating had truly taken their toll.

To make matters worse, my newfound freedom had me naively experimenting with new hairstyles and makeup, trying to discover my "look." Now I can see how the perm, the bad eighties hairdo, and the Madonna clothes were really *not* the most flattering of options. At the time, I had no clue and no one to tell me otherwise.

I did all I could to find myself, and along the way in the process, find someone to make me feel complete. I felt worthless without a guy and even more worthless when I couldn't land one. Without any support from friends or a significant other, I went it alone, and it went bad, very bad. I became miserable.

The old recordings started playing again in my head, repeating the same messages of doubt and fear. I kept hearing, "You're not good enough. You're worthless. You're a failure."

The shame resonated throughout my entire body, and I started to believe with every fiber of my being that I would never get a man. I really, really believed it. It was my truth.

One Friday night that fall, my roommates and I went out dancing at a local bar. As the designated driver, I took my responsibility seriously, so I had kind of a lame time because I didn't drink, and I didn't have the luxury of hiding behind an inebriated state.

While sitting at the bar alone, a guy walked over to me, pulled me out to the dance floor, and started to dance with me. I couldn't tell you what song was playing. I couldn't tell you what he wore, but I can tell you that my heart leaped about a mile. A guy pulled *me* to the floor and danced with *me*.

I felt so excited and had such a rush of worthiness and affirmation. I felt beautiful, loved, and wanted. I was so high on what was happening that I totally blocked out the reality of the situation.

He smoked a cigarette as we danced, and the lit end repeatedly hit my arms and burned my skin, causing me pain over and over. I looked past the disgusting smoke that he kept blowing in my face. After all, this guy liked me. Who couldn't deal with a little pain or a little smoke?

I didn't allow myself to see that he was being disrespectful. I didn't want to admit or believe he did anything wrong, no not at all. Every rational thought in my head that would have caused me to stick up for myself and walk away from the horrible situation was overridden by my misguided emotional high. Looking back on it now makes me feel so sad that I accepted this treatment, but I had. I was that much in need of attention.

When the song ended, he asked for my phone number, and I eagerly gave it to him. I watched him go back to his buddies at the bar, and that's when the world went into slow motion. His friends laughed hysterically, patted him on the back, and threw money at him as he crumpled up the piece of paper with my number on it and threw it on the floor.

He had won the bet, and his victory had been at the fat girl's expense. My feelings of worthlessness and the realization of my willingness to accept horrible treatment set in. I felt devastated, humiliated, and hurt beyond belief.

I went back to campus that night, swore off men, and lost myself in the comforting world of beer and potato skins. I threw myself into my studies. School gave me a sense of purpose; it was all I had left.

Fortunately I did have a few good attributes going for me. I was smart and a really good student. The grades came easy, and I hid in my books, finding comfort or solace in my academic achievements.

My grades had earned me a fairly prestigious on-campus job at the college computer center. In those days, very few of us had our own computers, and the college had just built a brand-new very high-powered computer center. They needed students to run the help desk, and I was asked to apply. This opportunity had only one problem: *the computer center was full of nerds.*

I had *really* wanted an off-campus job at the mall or waiting tables at a restaurant, but the computer-center job was easy, paid pretty well, and I didn't have to worry about transportation, so I took it. I figured I could deal with whatever personality conflicts came my way with the new group I would encounter while working.

Soon enough, I found a safe haven with my nerd friends. Like me, many of them had been social outcasts all of their lives. In our differences, we found incredible similarities and unity. An unspoken understanding, camaraderie, and fellowship tied us all together in our awkwardness. We became one big, happy, dysfunctional family. I learned to love nerds.

Natural relationship pairings happen in just about every family, and my new computer-center family was no different. I found myself attracted to one guy in particular, not because of his good looks or his smarts but because of his wounds. Legally blind from birth and recently dumped by his girlfriend, he desperately needed someone to listen to him and comfort him. I was glad to extend an ear and get involved in someone else's life for a change.

We soon entered into an exclusive dating relationship. We became inseparable, sharing stories until the wee hours of the morning.

Although highly functional, he had limitations due to his visual impairment. He needed someone to rely on for transportation, getting around, and for his freedom. He could see well enough to read but only if he held the print really close to his eyes. However, he couldn't recognize people from across the room, and he couldn't read a blackboard, even while wearing glasses. He could easily care for himself and was ridiculously smart, but anything that required going somewhere in a car or getting out of the house meant he needed a driver.

I remember the first time he told me he was blind and not able to drive. I thought, *Oh, your poor future wife. She'll always need to drive your daughter to ballet and do all the grocery shopping.*

Seriously, this very thought crossed my mind, and I let it go at that without any more consideration. Little did I know that a scant four years later, I would become that wife.

In the meantime, he had become my pet project and the focus of all my attention. How could I help? What could I do? What could I *fix?*

He graduated two years prior to me and got a fantastic local job. He then moved in with some friends. I might as well have been a fourth roommate because I seemed to be there all the time. I helped drive him to work, and I also made his lunch, arranged his schedule, did his shopping, and ironed his shirts. I went overboard, and he happily let me.

We got engaged my junior year of college, and he gave me a sparkly diamond ring, and I proudly wore it on my hand. My friends and roomies were all in awe. I became the talk of the dorm. I more than fit in; I was set for life. I had the coveted M.R.S. degree in the bag. I had become the girl everyone was envious of because I had landed a man and a ring and had set a date. I might as well have been the queen. I was hot stuff. *Me!*

No longer did feeling fat matter. No longer was I worthless. No longer did my bad hair or wardrobe mean anything at all. I was now "in," a card-carrying member of the "I Am Worthy Club" complete with a shiny trinket on my finger.

The wedding was planned, and both sets of parents were over the moon. I graduated, and we moved in together and prepared for our wedding.

Soon enough, the date was quickly approaching. I headed back to my hometown for a dress fitting three weeks before the wedding.

I won't even begin to go into the nightmare of the dress-shopping adventure. Suffice it to say that it was nothing like the reality shows where the bride-to-be walks in and has a hundred dresses to choose from and then walks out glowing and deliriously happy. With my size 26W physique, the options were very limited. My dress search was quite a bit more like "Call the tentmaker. Get some shiny fabric and some bows to throw on it. We're having a party."

On the day of the fitting, reality set in, and I stood there in the three-way mirror looking hard at myself. I thought I looked ridiculous, not because of my body or the gown, but because the two just weren't meant to go together. Not now. I knew deep down that I wasn't ready to get married. I knew he wasn't the guy. I knew I was getting married for all the wrong reasons, and I didn't want to go through with the wedding.

My mother and I left the bridal shop after the final adjustments were made, and we went out for lunch. I really wanted to discuss my concerns with her, but I was nervous about saying them out loud.

While we were deciding what to order, I took advantage of that silence to announce my doubts. "Mom, I don't think I want to get married now."

She looked at me over her menu from across the table and said, "Oh please! You just have cold feet. You'll be fine next week. Now, what are you having for lunch, the Reuben or the burger?"

I buried my head in my menu and ordered the hot corned-beef Reuben, my favorite sandwich ever. Biting into that crispy rye bread and feeling the pungent sauerkraut hit my tongue, I started the exercise of convincing myself that everything would be fine.

As it turned out, I was right. Our marriage was fine, or I should say I made it fine, at least for the first few years.

5
LIVING THE GOOD LIFE

Promise me you'll always remember:
You're braver than you believe, and
stronger than you seem, and
smarter than you think.

—A. A. Milne

y husband and I both worked hard, but we played hard too. I can't say that ours was a traditional relationship, but then again, I didn't have much to which I could compare it.

I had only that one relationship in high school, so my husband was the first and only serious relationship. As a result, comparing it to my parents' relationship was the only thing I had to go on. As newlyweds, what we had seemed to be enough.

We were best friends, and he looked to me for everything. I had a purpose, and he had a caretaker, so we both were satisfied.

I had just turned twenty-two, so as young adults with good jobs and making good money, we had a lot of fun. I literally dragged him everywhere, from around town to around the world. We went on adventures and day trips throughout the

United States, the United Kingdom, and Europe, skiing, hiking, eating, and sightseeing. I did all the booking, and he gladly joined in.

I could not have been happier. In addition to travelling extensively, I had many friends, and I ate at the best restaurants. Not caring about my size, my weight, or what I looked like was easy. My husband accepted me as I was, and I had no one else I needed to impress. Even though I wasn't happy with my body, I was so busy managing his life and our schedule that I didn't have time to think about my weight.

Additionally, I had formed a management consulting company right after we were married, and it had been developing a good client following. I loved working for myself. I was the boss, and my staff and colleagues respected me. I had a man. I owned a house and had money to buy whatever I wanted.

I thought, *Life is good.*

The high that accompanied my newfound status enabled me to distract myself once again from the reality of my underlying unhappiness. At home, things ran smoothly. We initially shared an equal division of duties, but over time I basically wound up doing absolutely everything. This wasn't because I wanted to or because my husband couldn't do it; I just found fault with *everything* he did and found that doing it myself was just easier.

No matter what the task, I could do it faster and with less hassle, and he could never do whatever it was as well as me. No one could. I barged in, needed to take over, be in control, and take charge of every aspect of our lives.

Looking back, I can see how I never allowed him to have an opinion, to take charge, or be responsible. I left him in a position where he was powerless. I was too afraid to give up that control.

All of these extra tasks exhausted me, but they also gave me a sense of purpose and accomplishment. Furthermore, they gave me something to complain about. I became the biggest martyr ever, just like my mother had done in her marriage with my father

How did my husband react to all of this? I guess he reacted like anyone in that situation would have. He shrugged his shoulders, stepped aside, let me *do*, and didn't complain. After all, what were his real choices? He could do the tasks and chores, but they would be completely wrong, and I'd complain. On the other hand, if he just let me do it, he didn't have to hear my complaints. All he had to put up with was my being Queen Martyr and repeating, "I do everything around here." These became our roles.

I patterned what I had learned from my parents' relationship and followed right into my mother's footsteps. Not only had I married a man with similar passive qualities as my dad, but my husband let me get away with and was complacent with my overpowering behavior.

He was content just like my father, who had also appeared satisfied. It worked for my parents, and I thought it would work for us as well.

The cycle repeated. I discovered over time that while that relationship style worked for others, it didn't work for me.

I had no idea at the time what a horrible precedent I had set and how detrimental it would be to my future. We as women are notorious for creating these types of situations for ourselves. We take over, take charge, and bully our way into browbeating our often very well-meaning husbands and partners into submission. We then become master martyrs for the next few hours, days, and weeks, and sometimes for the life of our relationships, all because we feel we have to do it all. Then we complain that no one is helping us and feel victimized.

We learn this from our parents' relationships, from our friends, and of course from the media. We're expected to be able to have it all, handle it all, and *do* it all. Of course we're not only expected to maintain these ridiculous standards, but we need to appear as if we're doing it all effortlessly—perfect hair, perfect body, perfect dinner, perfect life. It's as phony as an airbrushed model in a lingerie catalog. My life was no exception.

I was my own worst enemy and the one to yell the loudest at these injustices. This whole charade had paralyzed my man to the point where the only things he was really allowed to do was bring home a paycheck and take out the trash. I did everything else.

You name it, I did it. Gutters need to be cleaned? Sure, just let me get the pot roast in the oven first. Need more snacks? Sure let me run to the market and get you what you want. Don't worry, honey, you can take the trash to the curb after the game. I don't want to bother you while you're relaxing.

I was beyond handling it all, but it didn't matter to me. Remember, *I was in love.* My hubby *needed* me to do these things.

Taking care of everything was my mission, my purpose, my main focus in life, and my whole reason for living. I simply had *no* other choice. I felt *obligated.* My feelings of needing to portray the perfect life and my ability to rule it all were stronger than my impulses to ask for help, and so I did it with a smile on my face. After all, *I was fine.*

But I wasn't fine, not by a long shot. A few years into our marriage when the sparkle of travel and living the high life wore off, reality began to set in, and the consequences of my decision to get married hit me even stronger than it did right before I walked down the aisle. I became stressed out, miserable, and unhappy, and honestly, I had no idea why.

I blamed my discontent on my inability to handle everything. I had become overworked, overburdened, and I was responsible for way too much. I had a job and took care of all the financial arrangements needed to buy, maintain, and smoothly operate our house and everything that went on in it. I had done all of the shopping and all of the laundry, arranged all of my husband's transportation, prepared all of the meals, and planned all of the vacations.

Then there were our social obligations. I had planned and hosted fancy dinner parties, arranged our dinner schedules, hopped the party circuit, and made sure we maintained our appearance of being the perfect couple. Of course, impressing others was part of my workload.

As with the travelling, my husband happily joined me on the ride that was our life without much comment. I felt unappreciated, unloved, and just plain burned out. I drove myself crazy while at the same time driving him to the train station and myself to work. I was living my worst nightmare, and the worst part was, I didn't see that I was the one who had created it.

I started visiting a therapist at the time and discovered that I had an even bigger problem on my hands. Through talking it out with him, I was forced to face the realization that I wasn't really "in love" with my husband. I had to come face-to-face with the fact that I was really in love with being needed, and yes, it turned out that I really was codependent.

In my daily life, taking on all of the responsibilities enabled me to stay focused solely on my day-to-day activities. Keeping busy allowed me to avoid my reality and hide behind my obligation. The sense of worthiness I thought I earned was merely a façade, a cover from the fact that deep down I was still miserable, not in love with my husband, not loving my life, and certainly not loving my body.

I created a situation in my life where I could totally lose myself in everything else I did and not face my truth. I put on blinders and made myself believe that I had no choice other than to focus my attention one-hundred percent on everything that occurred in my marriage, my work, and my life.

I needed to keep all of these plates spinning in the air simultaneously. I felt I had to control everything around me so that I could feel in control of myself. Focusing on someone else and losing myself in my work was much easier than focusing on my problems. It let me convince myself that I was fine.

Instead of being proactive and delving more into the issues of my newly discovered codependency, I ran away from my therapist. I didn't want to face what I was up against, and consequently, I slid further into denial. I turned the other way and took on even more responsibility like it was a badge of honor. I rarely said no and joined just about every group and organization I could.

I buried myself even deeper in my busyness and my business and convinced myself that I was actually being productive and fulfilled. No problems here!

Let me tell you, people were impressed. I won awards, and I made a lot of money. Even my parents thought I was the best thing since sliced bread. I was recognized.

These rewards only added fuel to my fire. When people fluff you up and are impressed, you just want to keep doing more and more, so on I went keeping busy.

The accolades became addictive, and I thought I was on top of the world. I continued to avoid the truth of how unhappy my body, my marriage, and *my entire life* made me. It was all a house of cards.

Unbeknownst to everyone, inside I was starting to fall apart big time. The charade of keeping it all together was taking its toll. I had no idea what to do.

In 1999, after six years of marriage, I did the only thing a "good girl" could *possibly* do when faced with such overwhelming obstacles and feeling miserable about her body and her life. I got pregnant.

Up until then, I had pushed off having children as long as possible much to the dismay of both sets of our parents. I resisted motherhood like the plague, not because I didn't want to have kids or didn't like them; I was simply scared out of my mind to become a mom. My opinion of moms, well, was not good. I was petrified of becoming a bad parent and of repeating the cycle of shame and hurt that I had received growing up. Denying myself children seemed like the only way I could break the cycle of shameful parenting that had been transferred down from my Baba to my mom and I had assumed to me.

I clearly saw how the theme of shame and the damage it caused had crossed the generational lines in my family. I didn't want to pass along the same kind of suffering I had experienced as a child. I had it in my mind that I could not be different. It was my "curse."

Yet deep down, I was determined to be a different kind of mom. I wanted to be a better role model, and I wanted my children to grow up with a tremendous sense of self and worth as opposed to feeling less than. I didn't have any clue as to how to do that, though, so I simply avoided becoming a mom at all cost, that is until something in my heart told me otherwise.

I remember discussing going off the pill with my husband and actually trying to get pregnant. Although scared, I remarkably started to feel a tiny sense of comfort. I thought that maybe, just maybe through motherhood, I could create an environment where I could actually *belong.* Maybe our marriage would improve if we had a child to raise together, a baby who was *ours,* not "his" or "mine" like everything else had been.

I thought that maybe becoming a mother offered a greater purpose in my life. Maybe, just maybe I could break the cycle of bad parenting if I tried hard enough, if I read enough books, if I put my all into it.

I had only one stipulation, though. I wanted to be a mom *only* if I could give birth to boys. The thought of giving birth to a daughter scared the living daylights out of me. Who was I to be a mother to a girl?

My maternal instincts started to come to the surface. I now had another task to add to my list: becoming the perfect mom. So with a plan in hand, a focus in head, and a determination in heart, I got pregnant within a month after going off the pill. Twenty weeks later, right on target, I discovered I was pregnant with a boy.

With all of my plans in place, I gave birth to a happy, healthy child. I will never forget holding my son in the hospital on the night he was born. I looked at his angelic face with its wide-eyed innocence. Everything I had learned about being a mom during my pregnancy went out of my head like the air from a pricked balloon. All of my confidence simply evaporated. I felt overwhelmed and totally unqualified to hold his life in my hands.

Emotionally I was a mess. What had I done? I wasn't capable of being a mother to such a pure being. I knew I would screw up. I was doomed. All I wanted to do was cry.

Instead I made a pledge to him that very night that I would give him my all every day and that I would stand up for him and protect him unconditionally no matter what the cost. He would *not* go through what I did. *Ever.* I made a decision, and I was determined to stick to it.

His arrival also brought many changes to our household. We had lived as man, woman, and dog for eight years. All of a sudden a new being entered into our presence, and everything turned upside down, from sleeping schedules to work and everything else in between. From toys strewn all over the house to issues with the baby's car seat, nothing seemed to go right.

I now had more on my plate than I could even begin to handle. I felt exhausted, depressed, and could barely get out of the house as my son seemed attached to either my breast or his crib at all times. On top of that, my weight blossomed to two hundred seventy-five pounds. If I thought I was huge before the pregnancy, you can only imagine what I thought of myself afterward. I had become gi-normous, but I simply tried to ignore it. I had a baby to consider, so I couldn't focus any energy on myself at a time like this. I was breastfeeding, dammit. I needed to eat.

Funny how we can come up with excuses to hide our addictions and fears. Denial sets in quickly when we have what seems like valid reasons. After all, *I was fine.*

I can recall one luxurious evening when I didn't have to take care of the baby and was able to indulge quietly in a bubble bath. I drew the tub full of hot water, lit a candle, and lost myself in twenty minutes of hot, soaking bliss.

My contentment was short-lived. As I exited the tub, I caught a glimpse of myself in the mirror and just dropped the towel. As I looked at my reflection, I began to grab the rolls of fat around my mid-section, examining with disgust and shame the same belly that had so miraculously given birth only a short time ago. My body had gone from miraculous to monstrous.

Instead of appreciating the beauty of what I saw and appreciating the incredible and wondrous feat my body had been able to perform, I tore myself apart. Words of hatred, anger, and revulsion churned out of my head faster than ever. I cried like I have never cried in my life.

The image that stared back at me appeared to be nothing but fat and ugly. I looked and felt like the life had been sucked out of me (figuratively and literally through breastfeeding). I felt utterly hopeless and worthless and like a failure.

I realized I needed to get out and talk with other moms. I needed support and an ear to listen.

The hospital where I had given birth held a weekly meeting for new mothers from many walks of life. I went a few times, seeking support and an excuse to get out of the house. Unfortunately it didn't turn out to be the refuge I had hoped. I couldn't help but fall into the old habits of comparing myself to everyone around me. How did I stack up against the others? Was I a good-enough mom? Was I parenting properly? Was my baby's safety seat equipped with all the right bells and whistles? Did I use the right sterilizer? Was I hydrating properly?

It was neither a healthy nor productive environment for me as a new mom. Although the nurses were helpful, the group felt like one big competition among its members. I was convinced that there must be a "Mother of the Year Award" because everyone seemed to be trying to outdo the other. Many seemed to be there just to compare notes, offer unsolicited advice, and judge others.

Looking back I wonder how much of my perception was reality and how much of it was brought on by a hormonal fear we all surely shared as amateur moms. We had been thrown into a first-time experience, and I'm certain we were petrified of failing. When we find ourselves in such situations, it's easier to judge others as wrong in an attempt to make ourselves feel like we're doing right.

Regardless, the feelings of inadequacy for me were real, especially in my fragile, already-overworked physical and mental state. Every comment became a personal attack, not helpful advice. Every suggestion by the nurse coordinators further proved that I had no idea what I was doing. I felt inferior; I felt worthless.

I sat there in simple awe (and abhorrence), wondering how the hell these women made it to group without spit up on their shirts and looking so, well, damn happy, thin, and *perky* in their color-coordinated everything. They all had great post-baby clothes and plenty of wardrobe comments and compliments for each other.

On the other hand, my clothes and my style were not for complimenting. I'll remind you of the tough time I had simply getting regular clothes. Cute postpartum clothes were not an option for me. I had two looks: sweatpants with a flannel button-up top or shapeless pull-on elastic-waist pants with a nursing shirt complete with flaps that could have put a Boeing 747 straight to flight. They came in two fashionable colors: white and black, but with a baby, the white one didn't stay white for very long.

Weight, of course, was another hot topic within this group. For me, hearing about how breastfeeding caused the weight to fall off and how running around the school's track while pushing the right jogger stroller could get your ass back sounded like nails scraping down the chalkboard. Hell, I was more concerned with how to keep my ass from creeping around the front of me, let alone "get it back." All of it became overwhelming. What was supposed to be support turned into an anxiety-ridden episode that shone a spotlight on all of my "imperfections."

To make matters worse, group lasted a good couple of hours, so of course we were all encouraged to feed our babies while there. While others had no problem baring it all, I felt horribly self-conscious with the need to stay hidden and covered up, not because I was afraid to publically feed my child but because I was afraid of my size. Therefore, I wore my nursing shirt each time because it provided at least a little privacy while I nursed.

I was never more embarrassed than the day when I looked down and realized that I couldn't see my poor son's head attached to my nipple. My gi-normous body had failed me again. His poor little head was dwarfed somewhere under my oversized, swollen f-sized breasts.

I felt *mortified*. Even though no one ever said a harsh word directly to me, I made up stories in my head that they were all as equally disgusted with me as I was myself. While I'm pretty certain now that the story I had told myself was completely wrong (as most of the stories are that we tell ourselves), I bid farewell to the group that day and never went back. My shame was unbearable.

I then became what I jokingly refer to as a "hermit mom." I avoided most play groups and did a lot of solo activities with my son. I also worked *a lot*. I threw myself into a frantic, busy schedule and managed the house, my consulting business, my son's life, and my husband's life. But it wasn't enough.

A year and a half later, naturally the only logical choice was to have another child.

I pretty much sneezed and got pregnant. While I ended up experiencing a wonderful pregnancy, the stress of everything I continued to handle during this time started to have a greater effect on me than before. I was not nearly as agile as I had been during my first pregnancy. I couldn't mentally or physically handle as much.

While I wasn't considered too old to be pregnant at the age of thirty-two, my body was starting to catch up with me. Physically, I began to really struggle. I was on the cusp of becoming diabetic during this pregnancy because of my weight and the stress. Still I couldn't bring myself to ask for help from friends or family. I could handle it.

The last thing I wanted to do was expose myself. I had worked hard to make it look easy. I didn't want to be vulnerable and show anything but sheer perfection, so I suffered in silence.

My weight blossomed once again during this pregnancy, Growing along with my waistline were my feelings of shame, but still I trudged on.

Twenty weeks into my pregnancy, I went for my routine ultrasound. I was relieved to hear that the baby was healthy and growing according to schedule.

Then the ultrasonographer proudly announced, "It's a girl."

I reactively gasped in horror and started crying. She patted my shoulder and said, "Don't worry, Honey. She's perfectly healthy!"

I smiled, but the anguish was there. I became overwhelmed with guilt and shame at the horrible way I felt about being a mother to this perfect, unborn child.

Then anger took over my emotions. This time my worst fears were realized. Tears of anguish rolled down my face. The news devastated me and made me into a mess.

I knew I was a great mom to a boy. Boys were easy. Boys I knew. I had no problem with boys, but a girl? I was not prepared for a girl. I couldn't handle a girl. I had no doubt that I would screw it all up.

I *knew* deep within my bones how horrible the relationship between a mother and a daughter could be; I lived it. I wasn't ready for that.

I didn't want her to face the fears I had, have the issues I have, and I certainly didn't want to repeat the cycle of parenting that I had witnessed and to which I had become a casualty.

All I wanted to do was run away as fast as I could from the doctor's office, from my pregnancy, and from my life. After processing this news, I realized I couldn't do much more than wobble.

I was in trouble and needed help. My daughter was worth it. I was worth it, and I couldn't do it alone.

So I went back to therapy.

6
LETTING GO

"Some people believe
holding on and hanging in there
are signs of great strength.
However, there are times
when it takes much more strength
to know when to let go and then do it."
—Ann Landers

The pending entrance of a mother-daughter relationship into my life scared me like nothing else. I mean it really, *really* scared me. In hindsight, this pregnancy gave me the wake-up call I needed to springboard into, well, *my true intended life* and not the one I had been living.

I now found myself faced with taking on the role of a mother to a daughter, a role with which I had very little positive experience. I was being given an amazing opportunity to become the woman and the mother *I wanted to be*. Raising a child with a different style of parenting than I had previously known meant that I needed to start living life a whole new way, my way. It was time for a change of perspective. It was time for the *real* me to emerge.

My weekly visits to my therapist helped me see that maybe, just maybe I could channel my fear and my old beliefs into something truly productive and healthy. The work I was about to embark on could change my life if I was willing to explore the possibilities. There was one catch, though. I had to agree to face my fears head-on and learn to embrace a new way of thinking with an open heart and mind. I didn't have a doubt in my mind that I was ready, and I agreed to sign up for the program that very day.

At the start of my sessions I focused solely on my deepest fear, which was how to be an awesome mother to a daughter. Pretending that I had to contend with this single fear was easy. I convinced myself that it was the key, the answer to all of my other problems. So I put all of my effort and energy into fixing this one fear alone. I didn't see the need to deal with any other issue.

My therapist gently coaxed me beyond the blinders I wore. He helped me realize that I didn't have one issue but many issues that were woven together like an ugly, anxiety-ridden blanket of fear.

The more I looked at my worst nightmare, the more I became aware that so much more lay at the base of my fears. My therapist then encouraged me to dig deep and face *all* of my concerns. I couldn't fix one thing without uncovering some of the other ones.

We discussed self-love, self-acceptance, and my lack of both. We talked about the walls I had built around me and how I wouldn't allow myself to be vulnerable and open, even with my spouse or friends.

We discussed my lack of self-worth and self-belief. These feelings led me to realize that my concerns didn't lay in my ability to be a good mom but in my ability to break free of the cycle of bad parenting because I didn't love myself enough. I didn't feel worthy. I didn't let anyone in to help. Facing the path that lay before me was daunting.

As I moved along further in the therapeutic process, I really got worried. I knew that as soon as I opened the closet door to my life, everything from my past would come falling out in bushels. I had spent years stuffing my emotions, my fears, and my issues into that closet and had nailed that proverbial door shut. Then I had walked, no, ran away from it, not wanting to ever have to deal with anything in it ever again.

That running away and hiding from my problems served me well for a time, or so I thought. However when I looked down at my growing belly and imagined my beautiful daughter inside, I knew I couldn't keep that closet door shut any longer. I needed to throw it open and take a good, hard look at myself once and for all.

I believed I could do better. No, I *could* be better. I could be the mom, the woman, and the person I always wanted to be.

My goal in going through this process was not to judge or beat myself up any further. Years of doing that had gotten me nowhere. I needed to take a different approach, and I knew that working with a therapist, a trained professional was key.

I wanted to understand. I wanted to learn to love myself and let go of all of my preconceived notions of who I was. Now was the time to reinvent Stacey Hawkins or rather let the real Stacey emerge from the shadows where she had been silenced all her life. The only way to really accomplish that was to open the door and look inside, even if I didn't like what I saw. I needed to finally take a step back and look at *me*.

My therapist continued to encourage me. He reassured me that I didn't have to dredge up and tear apart every intimate detail of my life. I could simply examine it as a whole and then address only what I really needed to confront.

I had to look for the patterns of self-destructive behavior where I wasn't being true to myself. I then needed to force myself to look at how that had turned into the fears that had caused all of my roadblocks.

More significantly, looking at the past would give me a clear and present picture of where I was unhappy and why, and it would help me establish where I really wanted to go in my future. The purpose was not to torture myself with old hurts and not to point fingers or to blame or shame. It was to understand where and why I was stuck. That would be the information I needed to unlock the future.

This process would take work, and it would take sacrifice. I knew I would shed lots of tears and that I would have to open some old wounds and release some pain.

My determination to have a happy relationship with my daughter trumped everything, even my fears. I knew that I didn't want to relive my past in my present life and have the cycle repeat. Rather, I opted to revisit my past history with my therapist and put the "old Stacey" to rest.

In spite of all the work, I was given no guarantees. I knew the possibility existed to make some big changes and that if I stuck with it, the rewards could prove to be monumental.

I made a deal with myself. I would be as honest and as vulnerable as possible. I could no longer hide, and I could no longer stay in denial.

I was willing to do anything to be happy. My desire was that great. I had to just believe that I could do it.

I came across a quote from Henry Ford and taped it on my mirror so that I could look at every morning. It said,

"Whether you think you can, or you think you can't—you're right."

Once again, I stripped naked in front of the mirror. This time, though, I made myself not only look at the reflection staring back at me but to really *see* the woman standing before me.

I had to go beyond the tears and pain. I needed to acknowledge my body and the life in it for what they were— beautiful and powerful. I knew I had to look past the guilt and the shame, even if right at that moment I was only strong enough to do it briefly. I had to simply see what was really there and what could be.

Beaten, battered, and feeling an unprecedented combination of pain and deep love for my unborn daughter, I stared blankly back at my reflection, blinking hard. I tried to still the voices of shame in my head and not judge.

For the first time since I could remember, I felt an overwhelming sense of compassion for myself. Throughout my life I had judged myself so hard, always putting me last, making others more important, and trying to make everyone else happy. Over the years of giving, I had lost me, and I so desperately needed to give back to me.

Right now, I needed all the love, the compassion, the empathy, and the comfort I could muster. In that moment, the incredible benefit and gifts of love and acceptance for me and my body came to light.

I put my arms around my big belly the best I could. I rocked back and forth and took in a deep breath. I felt raw and exposed.

Finally and for the first time as well, I also felt a sense of hope. As I held myself, as I cradled my heart and my being, I felt love. When I looked again at the woman in the mirror, she smiled.

In that moment, I felt an amazing sense of power, determination, and strength come into my body. The word "enough" emerged from my lips in a whisper. I made a decision right then and there that I would do whatever it took to care for myself and my children and live my life to the fullest.

The quality of my decisions had determined the quality of my life up until that point, and I wasn't happy. I had created it, and I could create a way out. Nothing would stop me.

As I rested my hands on my pregnant belly, my purpose became crystal clear. I was done with feeling powerless, of just accepting what my life had become. I was done playing victim. Now was the time to make new and *better* decisions for *myself.* Now was the time to reclaim *my* life.

I had spent years evolving into a woman I didn't even recognize. I just went with the flow, never questioned anything, and allowed my life to be as such.

The good girl did as she was told. I had always followed the prescribed plan that society, my parents, my husband, and anyone else who had any influence in my life put in front of me. I soaked it all up like a sponge and *believed* those messages. I held those beliefs as gospel, as the truth, and I took ownership of them. What I believed about myself and the stories I was told all proved to be wrong.

I realized I had been programmed to believe I was the perfectionist, the one who had to meet everyone else's expectations, but in actuality I was completely different. I was the real, the fun, the bubbly, the it's-okay-to-screw-up me. The best part? I no longer had to buy into someone else's beliefs.

The day I had the epiphany that the rules *could be broken, that they could even be destroyed* was a turning point. I remember sitting in the coffee shop with a girlfriend when the realization hit.

We talked about how we grew up believing we had to be like our parents, to live up to everyone else's expectations. We talked about how unfair it all seemed and how we felt trapped and had no other choice.

In one of the most profound moments of my life, we both simply looked at each other and started laughing. We realized how ridiculous we sounded with the statements we were making and how very wrong we were. We had been duped by well-meaning people in our lives, and we could choose to think differently.

Our discussion caused a shift in my thinking, and I began to see that I did not have to be the good girl and do what I was told any longer. I did not have to be bound by the rules that had confined me. In fact in my conversation with my friend, I understood that I already had the freedom to rewrite the rules and the ideologies that I had been fed to believe. The truth was, I was *not* too big for my britches. I just needed a rule book and belief system that allowed me to be, well, me, and I had to be the one to write it.

I felt foolish for not realizing this sooner. Who didn't know that? What a simple concept. I found this revelation liberating, so freeing, and so enlightening. I had just never, ever thought about it. I had never questioned that life could be any other way than the way I was living.

When I discovered the *truth,* that I had the ability to start creating my own rules and have whatever I wanted, that I didn't need to accept what was or the status quo, then I knew that I could be who I really wanted and was intended to be. I knew darn well that this woman was vastly different from the one I had become.

It was time to forgive myself for being inauthentic to the one person who mattered most—*me.* It was time to let go of the anger I had and to release the blame and shame I felt all because I had not lived the life I had wanted to live.

I accepted that I had done the best I could with the knowledge I had. Now I knew I could do better; I could *be* better. In fact, I could do anything I darn-well pleased.

I remember putting my hand on the cool knob of the coffee shop door and opening it to head home. As I stepped across the threshold I excitedly thought, *Well, now what? How do I even begin to rewrite the rules and beliefs of my life? What* do *I want? I get to choose?* The prospect was thrilling and daunting at the same time.

I had been doing what I did for so long and getting nowhere that I didn't even know where to start. Yet I knew one thing for certain: the change *must* come from me. I didn't want to fulfill the adage that tells us that insanity is doing the same thing over and over again and expecting different results. I had been running long enough on the hamster wheel, and I needed to get off of it once and for all. I understood that if I didn't, I'd have no one to blame but myself.

I was free. I no longer had to play victim of my upbringing. With one cup of coffee and a conversation, I had released the goddess creator who would be in charge of determining my rockin' new life.

I possessed the determination, the desire, and the sense of purpose, all of which are the key building blocks for igniting the change process, but I needed more. Like a kid in a candy store full of excitement, I knew the possibilities were endless. I really had to think about what I wanted. Yes, me. What did *I* want?

For once, I put everyone else aside and thought about *my* life, *my* future, and *my* desires.

I knew I wanted to set some simple and basic goals to start. I just wanted to be happy, be a good mom, feel successful in my career, be a good wife, give back to my community, and most of all, truly learn self-love and self-compassion. All in all, I just wanted to feel like I was "enough." I wanted to breathe, feel joy, and happily live in the moment.

The problem was that even those basic needs seemed unattainable. I became overwhelmed as demanding and impractical thoughts raced through my mind. I had to lose ten pounds before I could love my body; I had to make more money in order to be considered successful; and I couldn't be happy in my life until my marriage was better. I panicked, and I froze.

This kind of stress was not uncommon for me. I frequently lost myself in a million different thoughts and took them down the proverbial rabbit hole of despair. The problem seemed to repeat for me as I took a thought and spun such an imaginary story around it that it dragged me down. Often when I got to the bottom of the rabbit hole I'd get so freaked out I wouldn't do anything; I'd just pick another project to get busy with and walk away.

This "analysis paralysis" is precisely what had kept me in the cycle of never getting anywhere and hating myself in the process.

This time, however, was different. My sense of purpose kicked into high gear. Undoubtedly my daughter's daily kicks from the inside helped, especially since each one served as a great reminder.

Instead of getting distracted, I got focused. I knew I needed to take small steps. I had to eat the elephant one bite at a time. I learned to stay in the present moment and not let my mind wander in all of the other directions it had previously gone in the past. Staying present, breathing, tackling one task at a time, and reveling in my accomplishments no matter how small were very important.

While every bone in my body wanted instantaneous change, a number of issues had to be unraveled first. I had to constantly remind myself that they took forty-plus years to obtain, and they were going to take time to get rid of as well. To expect them to go *poof* and disappear overnight was unrealistic.

I had to lean into the discomfort, to *feel* what I needed to feel, and then let it go. No more stuffing unwanted feelings in the closet.

Day by day I got organized. I put some simple systems into place, set some gentle-yet-firm timelines for myself, and simply started. I tried not to be a perfectionist about it.

My therapist had said that keeping the goal setting simple was important and that I should be realistic so that I could feel the fear and move forward anyway. I had no idea what lay ahead, but at least I felt a little bit in control.

In addition to getting my life in order, I also included fun things in my schedule. I took a pottery class. I joined a book club. I started putting money away for spa services and some weekend travel. I started exercising. Making time for *me* was something that I had avoided doing in my quest to take care of everyone else first. Practicing self-care would prove to be one of the most important parts of my journey, yet practicing it often made me feel guilty.

Undoubtedly, I was scared out of my mind. I had spent years, hell, decades shoving square pegs into round holes, creating, crafting, and carving my way into what I thought was my perfect life. If the peg didn't fit, I got a bigger hammer and pounded harder.

Why? Simple. It's what I thought I had to do because that's what I had been told and more importantly, it's what I was shown through the actions of the people around me. I knew no other way, and I didn't allow myself to believe that there *could* be another way. How wrong I was.

What I didn't realize was that there was a *real reason* the pegs didn't fit into my life: they weren't supposed to fit. When things don't seem to be working the way we want them to work, when we find ourselves facing uphill, insurmountable battles, it's because it's not supposed to happen that way. Sure, we can keep hammering away much like I did, but chances are pretty good that sometime in the future, you'll look back on the situation and realize it would have been better if you had just left it alone and accepted it as is.

Don't get me wrong. It's scary to let go and not force our lives to be the way we think it should be. Like most, I possessed a huge fear of the unknown. What would actually happen to me if I became the woman I wanted to be? I had no idea who she was or what my future would entail. I had to trust that my life would unfold exactly as it was intended to and reach way out of my comfort zone.

I wondered if letting go of some of my old beliefs would really change *me*. Would I lose my clients? What would my friends think? What would they say? Would people talk? How would my parents react? My kids? My husband? What would happen if these changes *in me* led to success with my business and I became wealthy?

What if I became famous and in demand? Could I balance it all? Could I be a good mom while running a big organization? Who was I to even dare think I could be that successful?

As my thoughts spiraled out of control, luckily my better sense took over. For the first time, rather than my mind running in spirals, I was able to recognize what I was feeling. I realized my old habits were kicking in. I was creating stories in my head once again and worrying about what "could" happen. I realized I wasn't living in the moment and following my heart. I realized my brain, and especially the little girl inside of me, instinctively wanted to play small, to keep my light dim, and just be silent. For a brief moment, I saw how those old feelings were more powerful than my gut instinct as I begin to worry once again about being too big for my britches. For a brief moment, I doubted myself.

One part of me said, "Come on, Stace, we don't really want to do this. We're *fine!*" The other part of me wanted to plow full steam ahead. In the confusion I felt full of conflict. I needed to think it through, to talk it out, but with whom?

That coffee shop conversation solidified the importance of having close friends with whom I could be open and share my most intimate thoughts. Through sharing and being vulnerable, I had learned a valuable lesson.

While I was never, ever afraid of being in the public eye, of being in the spotlight, or being the center of attention, I found one-on-one conversations difficult and scary. I had many acquaintances and very, very few true friends. I couldn't seem to make close friendships. I had no close relationships with family to whom I could turn. For reasons I couldn't understand, I wasn't able to turn to my husband either.

Creating intimate relationships, truly bonding one-on-one with people, and letting them into my world in a deep way was a challenge. I had a hard time trusting anyone. I felt lonely, scared, and afraid. I needed help and support. I needed a tribe. I needed someone who *understood*. I needed some real friends.

I knew that finding some sense of community with a new group would be a great way for me to let out my authentic self, so I accepted an invitation to a playgroup for children and their mothers that I had read about in a local magazine. Here, no one knew me, no one knew my "old" story, and no one had any expectations. For once, I could truly *be myself*.

I bought a new shirt to cover my pregnant belly, got a haircut, and made some brownies. Then one bright and clear morning, I headed off to this playgroup with my son. Little did I know, but participating in the playgroup would be the beginning of a whole new chapter of my life.

There, I began to forge relationships that forever changed me. With this new group of women, I actually started feeling like I was enough, like I was part of something greater than me, and like *I belonged.*

Here there was no judgment, only connection. They gave understanding, sharing, and common ground. My new friends offered unconditional love and friendship. They allowed me the freedom to be the woman, the mother, and the friend I had always wanted to be.

I started to look forward to the Tuesday playgroup. The time away from my lonely home life gave me a reason to get out of the house. It also gave me a reason to take a shower. With my new social interactions, I started caring about how I looked, how I dressed, and how I smelled. I wasn't looking to impress anyone, no, far from it. Instead, I really wanted to feel good about *me.* I wanted an excuse to put on some makeup and feel pretty. I wanted to feel like a girl.

Until that playgroup, my overwhelming thought had become *"Really? Why even bother getting out of my pajamas?"* I had fallen victim to the monotony and draining cycle of my work-at-home days, motherhood, and isolation.

As I started to expand my circle of friends, my hope started to expand. In fact, it blossomed even more. My confidence grew. I started to get excited about the direction my life was starting to take.

What also felt good, and I mean *really good* was finally belonging to a tribe. Something was very different about the two women who started this group, and I found myself drawn to them. In addition to the playgroup, we spent a lot of time together. They both lived very close to me, and our firstborn children were all boys born within six months of each other.

Although we were from different backgrounds, we all found ourselves struggling in one way or another. We stuck together and helped each another, free from judgment, free from criticism, and in an environment where laughter was always to be had.

For the first time I felt comfortable letting my guard down. I finally allowed myself to admit that I had trouble doing it all by myself, and then I allowed myself to "trouble" them for help.

Belonging to something greater than me and the little world where I had been living was wonderful. I had made new friends who created a support team of like-minded women. With them I understood I could finally soften my hard edges a little bit by letting myself be truly seen for who I was becoming. The whole experience gave me a sense that I was on the right path, and I was happy.

In addition, my continuing sessions with my therapist had me feeling good about my daughter's approaching arrival, and my plan was in place for when it happened.

Every day I took small steps toward, well, I wasn't exactly sure *where* I was going, but that didn't really matter. I may have moved very slowly, but I was heading in the right direction toward being the mom and the woman I wanted to be.

The confidence and fire incited by feeling good about myself lit me up so much that my goals started to come into reach. I *felt* like a good mom. I *felt* beautiful. I *felt* like I had a purpose with my friends and that I was giving back. That sense of community, of belonging, brought my true self to the surface, and I shined. Feeling this way was wonderful.

Not long afterward, my two BFF's and I found ourselves delivering baby girls within a few months of one another. Much rejoicing was experienced by all.

Life as I knew it was really changing, and this time around, the change was good.

7

WAKE UP!

"Do you want to know who you are?
Don't ask. Act!
Action will delineate and define you."
—Thomas Jefferson

I'll confess. Although I was super excited about changing my situation for the better, the addition of a new baby into the household once again turned things upside down, to say the least.

The extra responsibilities only compounded my stress. Before long, the physical as well as the mental exhaustion set in.

To make matters worse, we had moved into a one-hundred-fifty-year-old home that needed almost complete and total remodeling. My husband couldn't contribute much in the way of handiwork, if anything. He worked a full-time job in New York City, which required a three-hour round-trip commute.

Consequently, I had not only added new mom to my to-do list, but I also became head contractor, transportation coordinator, and chief care-giver, not to mention I still worked as CEO of my business management company. My head spun like never before.

I took a deep breath, closed my eyes, and tried to look through all of the clutter to see the promise of the future in front of me: new baby, new house, and new attitude on life. The possibilities were limitless.

With my eyes opened, however, that vision blurred greatly. My house and my newly tested parenting skills seemed to be in shambles.

My daughter became very colicky, making my life completely different from the easygoing days with my infant son. No matter what I did, I couldn't soothe her incessant cries and high-pitched screams. The incidents were undoubtedly painful for her and nerve-wracking for me.

Late nights ended up with her sleeping attached to my nipple and me seeking similar soothing through anything I could put in *my* mouth for comfort. I became a slave to her needs, simply because I wanted peace for her, for me, and for the rest of the family.

In my mind, I didn't think I could make anyone happy, and of course my self-care suffered. I assumed my husband and son resented the extra time I spent caring for my daughter's needs, even though they never said so or complained.

In the morning, both guilt and shame overcame me when I needed to leave my children with caregivers so that I could go to work. Then the guilt increased after dropping them off because of the joyous relief I experienced due to the resultant peace and quiet. Getting to the office did nothing to alleviate my remorse. I just knew that my work and clients suffered because of my exhaustion and inability to focus on my job.

By the time I got home at night, I was fried mentally and physically. I beat myself up even more because I couldn't get dinner on the table. On those nights when I was actually able to prepare something, it was either frozen meals, something microwaved, heat and eat out of a box, or one of the same boring meals like chicken and vegetables that I seemed to be making over and over to simply to fill the void. I couldn't even nourish my family well. I felt like a total failure.

To make matters worse, my house couldn't provide a safe haven of peace and solitude. Our renovation created a constant flood of construction workers in our home, sometimes for twelve hours a day, seven days a week. Sheetrock dust covered everything.

Old houses were known for lead paint, which could have been anywhere. The possibility that it existed in my home with little kids around was added pressure. For what seemed like forever, I had no kitchen. I washed dishes and baby bottles in the bathtub, often while taking a shower.

The disruption of it all was stressful. It was chaotic. The pandemonium under my roof was matched by the pandemonium that ran through my head and my body. I was a mess and didn't know what to do.

In the midst of it all, I simply tried to breathe, stay present, find peace where I could, and rely on my little tribe of new friends. I continued to believe in myself and in the process. I was told the journey would not be easy, and the experiences all around me were putting me to the test. I forced myself to remain focused.

Frustrated yet determined, I knew this was all part of my master plan, that things were unfolding just the way they were supposed to whether I liked it or not. If I could survive these obstacles, I could survive anything.

However, I'll admit that I did feel totally, and I mean totally out of control. While I truly understood that so much was out of my control and that I just needed to let it go and not worry about them, I also knew I could do some things to make my life a little easier.

The first thing I did was dissolve my business consulting practice. Although I had grown quite successful over the years, the business environment I was in was changing. The time seemed right to finish up projects with my few remaining clients and close the doors for good. These clients still had quite a bit of time left in their contracts so I still had some work to do for the next year, but I took on no one new. My husband was supportive, and I was rather pleased and a bit relieved that I would be able to care for our children full time. Of course watching my business disappear was sad, but I knew it was the right thing to do.

I decided to be proactive and harness the power of organization. Having a small sense of control over my environment, accomplishing tasks I knew I could, and achieving small goals gave me a sense of fulfillment and pride.

I looked at my schedule, the kids' schedule, everything I had to do, and the things I *wanted* to do, including fun and take-care-of-me kind of things. I put them into a pile, organized them, and put a daily system into place. It didn't seem like much, but it was a start. It made me feel like I had managed to get a handle on things so that I could keep on track with my goals for the future.

Once again, I practiced self-care first. I got up early and showered and dressed. I had made lunches the previous night so that we would be ready in the morning. I got the kids to daycare on time with a smile on all three of our faces. I didn't feel guilty anymore about enjoying the peaceful car rides to visit my few remaining clients. I got focused at work after delegating duties and didn't feel guilty doing so.

I started asking for additional help. I employed a woman to clean my house a few times a month. I hired someone to mow the lawn. Summers brought me an amazing au pair and her family from Germany, who have since become lifelong friends. I went grocery shopping once a week and started planning and making dinners.

I stopped complaining about what wasn't working and started taking action to make things happen in a better way. I had learned that things could be better if I made better decisions and then acted on them. When we know better, we do better.

I wound up taking my pain and the lessons I'd learned along the way, especially those recently, and channeling them into an easy-to-follow system that could help others create purpose-rich and rewarding lives as well.

The work involved was well-worth the rewards, and the end justified the means. The steps I had laid out before me in my system were simple. As long as I stayed focused, present, and determined, they became easier.

Dedicating myself to sticking to the program on a daily basis undoubtedly proved challenging at times. I knew, though, that if I took action and kept moving forward, every day I would get a little closer toward reaching my bigger goals. I would attain the happiness, the fulfillment, and the self-love that had seemed so elusive.

I started smiling more. I started stressing less. I started to actually lose weight and love myself even more.

Impulsively, I wanted everything to happen overnight. Realistically, I knew I needed to keep pace minute by minute. Whenever I hit a stumbling block, I rehearsed one of my favorite quotes:

"When you take care of the minutes, the hours
take care of themselves."
—Lord Chesterfield

I applied this saying to everything and every aspect of my life and practiced living it every waking second of every day. It kept me present (and still does).

I focused on myself, what I wanted, what I needed to do each day, and living moment to moment. I had no hard and fast deadlines. I was embarking upon a journey, not a destination.

My coaches and practical experience taught me that the work required to stay in this frame of mind would be a lifelong process. While setting goals and milestones is important, the desire for happiness and fulfillment is never-ending and always changing; therefore we're always a work in progress.

It's not that the process has to be exhausting, nor do I mean to imply that you're back on the hamster wheel trying to find something that's unattainable. The lesson to be learned is that you never get to that point in time where you get to the top of the mountain in your life and say, "I've arrived. I'm done."

Life is a constant flow of energy. It's always moving and is to be enjoyed every day. We never come to the point where we "arrive."

The fortunate person understands that she shouldn't hold any expectations other than to be happy and blissful. She understands the importance of moment by moment.

Again there is no final destination when it comes to doing the work needed to live your best life. The harsh reality is that the only final destination is death.

That eye-opening notion hit me hard. When I saw so clearly that no matter what I did or who I tried to please, make happy, or give the last breath of my being to, I was no different than anyone else. I too would die alone. *That* motivated me like nothing else.

I didn't want to die knowing that I lived *my* life for everyone else and not me. I may die alone, but come hell or high water, I would die happy, fulfilled, and I would leave a legacy of happiness behind me. *That* was the only thing I knew I had *total* control over.

8

SHOCK

"Out of the mouth of babes ...
hast thou ordained strength ..."
—Psalms 8:2

The thought of leaving behind an unfulfilled life haunted me. While I have never had a near-death experience, the thoughts of dying and its inevitability propelled me forward, and they continue to do so to this very day.

Shifting into this type of big-picture thinking forced me to look at things for what they really were and not what I *wished* them to be. My reality was that I was making progress and feeling better physically about my environment, but part of me was still quite unhappy. I knew the relationship with my husband had everything to do with that.

The stress I felt in my marriage combined with the fact that I didn't think I really deserved much better for myself at that time also contributed to my being chronically overweight.

I wasn't in a place where I felt strong enough to start facing the big issues related to my marriage. Instead I decided to focus on my weight and healthier cooking. I wanted to get involved in a positive project that would take my mind off my misery.

So I dove headfirst into figuring out how to make fast, healthy, and tasty meals with little work or effort. Like most of us, my body and taste buds had been programmed to love fat, salt, and sugar. If I was going to take all of these things out of my food, then I needed to put flavor back *in* it.

I started trying all kinds of new recipes, experimenting with flavors and spices, and developing recipes of my own that tasted great. I took a class on healthy cooking at the Culinary Institute of America to get some basics under my belt.

One thing led to another, and before I knew it, I had all of these bags of spice blends that I had concocted. I used them to whip up foods that tasted great.

One day one of my girlfriends offered me ten dollars for a bag of the "garlic stuff." I knew I was onto something. In the back of my mind, I started thinking about a business plan.

On a whim and before I put together a serious plan, I decided to create a small product line and test the waters to see if anyone would be interested. I met with a few spice vendors, filled my little car with some bulk spices, and blended together my top-ten spice concoctions in a brand-new cement mixer. (Yes, the same kind constructions workers use.) Since it wasn't Food and Drug Administration approved for spice processing, I bribed the local auto-body repair shop to coat the inside of the mixer with food-grade paint so that the mixer could go from a piece of construction equipment to my spice blending machine.

I went online and ordered a pallet of three thousand beautiful glass jars from Italy and had them shipped to my home. When the tractor-trailer arrived with them, we discovered it couldn't drive up my quarter-mile-long driveway, so it had to park at the end. We had no way to take the pallet out of the truck without a forklift, and the truck driver didn't have one.

I was shell-shocked. What was I going to do? At that time, I truly questioned whether or not I had a clue as to what needed to be done to start this possible business.

The truck driver was patient and more than kind. (I also think he thought it was all rather humorous.) I stood there with eyes wide open trying to imagine how I was going to solve my problem. Then I remembered a construction equipment rental center was less than a mile up the street.

I drove to the rental center and quickly told the manager my plight.

"You're doing what?" he asked.

He applauded my entrepreneurial thinking but told me that since I wasn't a contractor, I couldn't open a construction account, and he couldn't bill me for his services. He then pointed at me and with a joyful twinkle in his eye said he would personally drive a forklift to my house, unload the pallet, and put it in my garage in the next fifteen minutes. The catch? In exchange all I had to do was make his staff lunch with some of my spices that week. I was overjoyed.

I spent the next few weeks getting my products ready to go. Labels were made, the jars were beautiful, and I sent out flyers for an open house tasting party.

At that event, I sold every jar I had made. People raved about the food. Everyone wanted recipes and more products than I even had available. I knew I was onto a concept that could be really good.

My business dreams, however, would have to wait. The stresses in our marriage had taken their toll, and tensions ran high. After years of living codependent lives, we were both filled with resentment and unspoken anger toward each other. Having children changed the dynamic of our relationship and shifted my energy from caring for him to caring for them. It was a change for which he was not prepared.

All throughout our relationship, I had willingly, yet unknowingly, made my husband dependent on me. Then when I couldn't care for his every need any longer (and he refused to do things for himself), I simply lost all respect for him. Instead of having two children, it turned out I really had three.

I truly *wanted* to change my mindset and respect him as my husband. I also wanted him to understand my perspective and that I needed help, not resentment. We spent over two years in marriage counseling, countless hours of talking, attending workshops together, and I was still in therapy trying to fix me. After being together for sixteen years, I had hoped we could learn to do things differently, but I'll be honest. I was skeptical.

I'll never forget one of our last visits to the counselor. After listening to my husband complain about how he didn't see how he could do anything more to be helpful, the counselor lowered his glasses to his lap and slapped his hands on his thighs.

In a very loud voice, he said, "My God, man, would you please give this poor woman a break?"

In the end, even the counselor said our marriage was hopeless. I felt horrible about the situation I had created where I had allowed my husband to be so dependent on me. Yet while he had been given every opportunity to finally do things differently, he still refused to let go of his own fears. He didn't want to be the man our children and I needed him to be. He was happy with our old arrangement.

However, I needed a change. I didn't want the marriage that my parents had had any longer. I was done.

In anger and frustration, my husband told me that if I thought the grass was greener on the other side, then I should try to find a new man. If I found the right guy, he'd agree to a divorce.

I repeated his words back to him for verification and to clearly understand that he meant I was free to date other men while we were still married.

He agreed and added, "You'll never find anyone who will put up with you. Good luck."

I consulted a lawyer that week and began to investigate options for a separation.

I believe he didn't think I would actually call him on his bluff, but out of a combination of spite and curiosity, I figured, *Why not?* I didn't hesitate to take advantage of the opportunity he presented. Thus began my pursuit for "Mr. Right."

Online dating had become popular, and I flipped through the pages like a Sears catalog at Christmas and imagined the possibilities. I went on a handful of coffee dates and was unimpressed.

What I found fascinating, though, was the vast number of people who were going through similar, major relationship changes. Every date I went on seemed to be a tale of divorce and heartache. My "dates" turned into more of a social get-together out of the house and became less and less about a search for romance.

Then I met *him*—the tall, dark, and handsome window tinter who "drove" into my life in his shiny fast car and swept me off my feet. Going through a bad divorce himself and in need of a companion, we shared our misery and found great comfort in one another, mentally and physically. We needed each other and gave one another purpose and meaning. I felt so good about helping him and being there for him throughout his difficult divorce. He awakened my yearning to be feminine by making me feel alive, wanted, pretty, and desirable. I flourished.

I didn't realize how desperate I had become to get out of my marriage over the years. This new relationship brought it all to light but not in a healthy way. Unfortunately, my desperation threw me from one codependent relationship right into another. Instead of looking at my window tinter as a new partner, I saw this man as my knight in shining armor, my savior, and the one who would *fix* everything by rescuing me. I was stuck on him like the instant cling window film he hung for a living.

I became devastated when he ultimately ran in the other direction as far away from me and our relationship as he could go. While our long-term togetherness was not meant to be, the lessons I learned about who I was, the power I truly had as a woman, and the determination to find my own perfect match were solidified. But I was afraid.

I knew there was no turning back from my separation with my husband and that I needed to leave him once and for all. All indicators pointed in that direction, but I just couldn't find the nerve to do it. To make matters worse, I knew my husband would never be the one to leave me. He was too dependent, too needy, and too afraid of living on his own. One dramatically eye-opening event was all it took for me to finally do what was right for all of us.

On a bright school-day morning, my husband, eight-year-old son, and six-year-old daughter went through the normal motions of the busy weekday routine that started with breakfast. My husband stood at the stove making eggs for himself and dropped something, making a mess.

I instantly chided him with one of my typical snide remarks about how careless he was, what a mess he had made, and that I hoped he didn't expect me to clean up after him. I was nasty. He had no time to reply.

From across the kitchen we watched as our adorable little daughter stood up from the table, hands on hips, and repeated back my very words to her father, scolding him in the exact same tone and using the same words as I had. I was shocked and had the wind knocked out of me.

It was as though a huge mirror had been placed in front of me. In that instant, I realized how detrimental my actions had been, not just that morning but throughout her entire existence.

What kind of a role model had I portrayed as a woman and as a mother? Was I teaching my daughter to act the way I did with her future husband? Was I exemplifying the loving, kind woman I wanted her to be? Was that how a wife was supposed to act? My mind raced.

On the flip side, what was I teaching my son about the kind of relationship he was supposed to have with his wife? Was this how I wanted him to be treated by women? Was it okay for him to be cruelly disrespected by his wife? In that instant I saw what horrible lessons I had taught my kids by example. I felt sick to my stomach.

I took one look at her, and I knew I wanted to totally change my life. I needed to set my husband free so that he could be the man he wanted to be. I needed to allow myself to be the woman I wanted to be, and my husband and I to become better role models for our kids. There was no other choice.

When I saw the model of a poor relationship we had given our children, the definitions we had put into their heads about the roles men and women should take, and how to act and live by our dysfunctional example, I crumbled. The reality was that my kids would grow up following in my footsteps and completely repeating the process I worked so hard to break if I didn't do something.

I had broken the cycle of shameful parenting, but I had a lot to learn about how not to be a shameful wife. I was motivated but petrified. I was unsure of where to start. I had no divorced friends to whom I could talk. I couldn't go to my parents. I just didn't know what to do.

I needed to clear my head and find a place to start. After getting everyone out of the house that morning, I sat outside on the ground, leaned back, hands in the grass, face in the sun, and just stared at the Hudson River stretched out before me. Without thinking, I started talking to the sky. Anyone who saw me would have thought I was crazy.

I put my needs out there to the clouds and the flowers and the river. I'm not sure I even realized what I was doing at the time, but I didn't know what else to do. While I'm not a religious woman, I've always found solace in nature. So sitting where I was made me feel grounded and helped me with sense of clarity and calming my fears.

I started talking, thinking, crying, and opening my heart. I wasn't necessarily looking for answers, merely wanting to get things off my chest. Exhausted, I closed my eyes to the sun and breathed deeply, enjoying the moment of silence.

Imagine my surprise when I heard a voice in my head say, "Breathe and move forward. *Trust and believe.*"

I began to paint a whole new picture for myself. I envisioned a world where I was at a healthy, ideal weight; my kids were happy; I was a great role model; we traveled as a family; I made a steady income; I found true love; I drove a new car; etc. I wasn't looking at a few things to fix; I was looking at a major overhaul.

The three challenges I had to overcome were also the largest. I needed to lose a hundred pounds; I needed to figure out how to turn my hobby into a business; and after seventeen years of marriage, I needed to get divorced. I was done. That much was clear.

The prospect of doing this all at once scared the living daylights out of me. But this time was different. This time I allowed myself to feel the fear but move forward anyway. I wanted change, and it could only happen from me.

I recognized that little voice inside my head that tried to sabotage so much of what I wanted to have, to do, and to be in life, and I wanted to ignore it. That little voice of fear screams loud, sometimes to the point of paralyzing us from doing, well, anything. I was determined to get past that fear once and for all and get on with making decisions based on what felt right for me. I wanted to make choices based on gaining pleasure in my life, not decisions based on wanting to run from pain.

I was not afraid to live on my own, though. I might as well have been living alone all those years, having assumed all of the household duties, driving my ex and the kids around, and juggling our finances.

I was scared to death of the unknown and not knowing what to do with myself and of *not having to focus on anyone else but me*. After my husband left, I had no one left to fix. Instead I had all the time in the world to spend working on nothing but *me*.

Initially my parents were less than supportive. In fact upon announcing my pending divorce, my mother said to me, "Well, *now* what are you going to do?"

My response was simple. "I guess now I have to take out the garbage too."

I knew my mother's reaction came out of her own fear and worry about how I would handle living alone and taking care of two young children. I refused to accept her fear as mine; rather I took in a deep breath, trusted in myself and my decisions, and took action steps to get divorced and change my life. No one would stop me from having the life I wanted and deserved. This time, I would listen to no one else's advice except my own. Although trusting my gut was a bit scary, it was exactly what I knew I had to do. That sense of trust would turn out to be one of the greatest gifts I have ever received.

I found a relevant quote by Madisyn Taylor that said, "We develop grace as we learn with the guiding hand ... [that] life will unfold exactly the way it should."

I printed out this quote and hung it in a few places in my house, including on the top of my computer where I'd see it every day. I put my plan into place, focusing on controlling what I could and leaving the rest behind. I knew that I could only worry about what was in front of me. Who was I to worry about anything else?

Every day as my life started unraveling and then coming back together, I believed more and more that I was doing exactly what I needed to do. On my journey, something even greater happened. I started to truly *believe* that I deserved and was worthy of the strength and the gifts that came my way daily. Some gifts were tangible like dinner invites from neighbors, and some were intangible like the happiness and comfort I received from others when I felt down. Seemingly, "someone" had listened to my request for assistance.

My divorce was soon drafted, and my husband moved to New York City. After he left I was forced outside of my comfort zone. I needed to start asking for even more help with the kids and the house, which was a *huge* taboo in my world. I grew up with the belief that you *never* asked for help. Although I had made some progress in that area, I still considered reaching out to be a sign of weakness and fault. I hadn't yet quite gotten over the belief that you needed to do it yourself no matter what the cost.

So finding myself alone and physically and mentally unable to handle the responsibility myself, I had no choice. If I was going to survive with no family around, I needed to lean more on my friends for help. To my surprise and shock, they were incredibly happy to lend a hand.

I realized that my limiting belief of asking for help all these years was yet nothing more than another untrue story I had made up and told myself. This was pointed out to me in a rather eye-opening exchange.

One day a friend had brought home both of my kids from a party. I expressed my sincerest thanks to her and confessed that I felt like a failure because I couldn't pick them up myself.

Her response struck me. "Stacey, you know how good you feel when you do something for someone, and they appreciate it?"

I nodded in affirmation.

She continued. "You know how crappy you feel when you *want* to do something for someone, and they refuse?"

I nodded again, knowing exactly how that rejection felt.

"Who are you to deny me the pleasure of doing this for you?" She then chuckled.

In that moment, I saw how I had rejected people around me for years by turning away their help. Although help was what I really needed, I felt "less than" for accepting it. Rather than creating a win-win situation where I got what I needed, and they felt good giving it to me, I pushed countless people away as I tried to be Wonder Woman.

Reflecting on this *aha* moment, I didn't allow myself to feel shame as I normally would have. Instead, I took the epiphany as a valuable lesson and vowed to *never, ever* act that way again.

A tremendous amount of grace comes your way through the simple acts of creating your tribe and accepting help. Receiving with appreciation and gratitude, being truly grateful for what is coming your way, and practicing that gratitude on a daily basis often offsets the feelings of less than. When we are truly thankful, only then can we begin to appreciate the joy of receiving what those around us so desperately want to give.

Building my tribe, confiding my imperfections and my inability to handle it all, and getting downright vulnerable turned out to be one of the best things that could have ever happened to me. Understanding that other people were in the same boat as me was so potent and life-changing. We all try really hard to keep it all together, to make it look perfect, to do it flawlessly, yet we are stressed beyond belief trying to achieve everything we think is expected of us. Then we are left feeling like total failures when we can't make it happen.

This knowledge would be key in my decision to open my life and write this book. I wanted others to know that we are all the same. None of us, no matter how wealthy, pretty, smart, tall, etcetera, are immune.

We are all human. We have all been programmed in much the same way, and we all feel some sense of insecurity.

Nothing is more powerful than someone putting an arm around you and saying, "Me too, sister. I've been there, and I understand."

9

Pulling It All Together

"It takes courage...
to endure the sharp pains of
self-discovery rather than choose to take
the dull pain of unconsciousness that would
last the rest of our lives."
—Marianne Williamson

Although I had help, I was still stressed out.

I had lost weight and had kept it off for some time, but the additional strain had taken its toll. Before I knew it, the stress had led me back to emotional eating for comfort. My weight blossomed once again.

I needed to get back on track with food and with cooking and feeling good about feeding my kids. I knew I had to pull my spices out of the box and really start cooking once again. All of my years of dieting and practical knowledge told me one thing—what you put in your body is what you'll get out. If I wanted to feel good, I had to put the good stuff in and get rid of the garbage. It was that easy.

I became vigilant, but I also knew I had to be kind of sneaky with my children. Kids can be really opposed to change. I knew that if I made a big announcement that Mission Healthy Food was starting, I'd be greeted with eye rolls and resistance. So I took it slow and steady.

I threw myself into cooking. While I had always been a decent cook, like most working moms I just didn't have time. I knew there had to be a better way to prepare good food and not have it take so long.

Through trial and error, I started creating and cooking more and more amazing meals in just minutes. My kids loved what I fed them, and the meals made me feel physically better. The mental cloud lifted, and my energy level soared.

Over the course of a week, I went through the pantry, the fridge, and the freezer and eliminated those things that were just "horrible," such as baking mixes with hydrogenated oils, packaged frozen foods with unrecognizable ingredients, and sugary drinks. I swapped them out with healthier alternatives.

I knew the importance of increasing the veggies and almost totally eliminating refined carbohydrates from my diet. Since I had been diagnosed with and battled a thyroid disorder since my daughter was born, I had learned firsthand how gluten and carbs were well-known causes of inflammation and can wreak havoc on the body. I needed to address these detrimental foods as well.

On the other hand, I knew that really good carbs were important to both the kids and me. At this point, though, I wasn't exactly sure which foods contained the good stuff and which ones were the offenders.

I started eliminating all processed carbs and anything with wheat or gluten. Over time, I reintroduced whole grains and good carbs like sweet potatoes and squash. Within just a few days of getting started, I felt great.

When I reintroduced bread, though, that's when my body reacted violently. I was plagued with stomach cramps and digestive problems. Sleepiness became the norm anytime I ate foods with gluten. Recognizing this as a problem food for me, I resolved to continue with a whole–foods-based diet that was rich in protein and vegetables, lower in glycemic index, and gluten-free. Realizing this didn't leave me with my *normal* range of foods to eat, so I began to think outside the box.

To meet my goals of eliminating the crap from our food, everything needed to start with whole ingredients that were closest to their natural state. That meant good protein sources like chicken, fish, shellfish, and beef, and alternative sources like beans and grains, and lots of fresh veggies.

From that point on, I used simple cooking techniques, tried-and-true recipes but with a new spin, and of course, FLAVOR. That's where my products made all the difference. They proved to be the key to making fast and easy food that tasted good no matter what I made.

Making dinner became *so easy.* Mixing and matching the spices with simple whole foods became fun. Even the kids got in on it. We experimented by adding vegetables, changing things up, and thinking of new ways to cook.

My food choices turned out to be the key for my long-term weight loss and overall health. I started looking into commercially prepared diet programs for additional help and ideas. They seemed to mirror what I had discovered about lowering carbs and increasing fresh produce.

I needed some help with calorie restriction and structure in my own diet. I tried a few of these programs and found great success.

In joining several of the online communities, I learned quickly that many people who went on similar commercial diet programs were not as successful as me. Further investigation showed that because they quickly got very bored with the foods they ate, they went back to their old eating habits, falling off the program. I contribute my success to learning how to cook so many recipes that tasted great and complied with the diet. The secret was my spice blends.

I knew then what I know now, and that's when we're bored, when we're sick and tired of eating the same things, and when we eat things that don't taste good, soon enough we get discontented and dissatisfied, go back to old habits, and pack on the weight.

I wanted to do everything in my power to keep the weight from coming back on again. I wanted to ensure success and be able to create foods that I would want to eat for the rest of my life. I knew that a world of flavor was waiting for me if I put my skills to the test.

My friends became my recipe guinea pigs and my biggest cheerleaders. I'll never know if my tribe simply loved my products and taste testing my meals or if they truly were my best fans. (I'm going to say it was both.) However, through them I found the courage, the strength, and the encouragement to press forward with my cooking and with my ideas to relaunch the product line into a full-fledged business.

I also had to look at the realistic changes that were happening in my life. I now faced big bills, no quality time with my kids, and stress beyond stress. If I could get this business off the ground, I might be able to get out of debt, have at least some flex time with my kids, and be doing something I truly loved.

I considered the possibility that maybe, just maybe if I put my efforts into the business wholeheartedly, then I just might be able to create something that could be a win-win for us all.

My weight dropped pound by pound. My excess body fat literally started disappearing without a lot of effort. My skin glowed, my body felt *alive*, and the kids ate almost anything I put in front of them.

I was happy, the kids were happy, and life was good. The work I did in the kitchen wasn't just for my family; it was also research and development for my business.

People began to notice changes in me and the kids. We were not as harried, and the kids were healthy and also glowing. More importantly I was losing weight and smiling. I'll never forget the day one of my friend's husbands called me hot (yes, and thankfully in front of her). I knew that I was doing something right.

Not only was my physique changing for the better, but I felt like such a great caregiver to my family. I knew that what I fed them was *good* for them. What was even better was how they started complimenting my cooking. Hearing their praise was an awesome feeling that could be rivaled by no other.

The trickle-down effect of making dinner every night was immense. When we could, we actually sat down at the table and ate together. When we couldn't, I had the power and the knowledge to make a meal that we could still eat no matter who came home when.

The benefits of spending time with my kids and the health benefits of clean eating were nothing short of incredible. I saw how powerfully transforming something so very simple could be, not only for me but for hundreds, if not thousands of others as well.

I took my recipes and turned them into a cookbook and then into two cookbooks and then three. With so many versatile ideas and so many ways to transform simple foods into great meals, I was on fire, and I continue to be.

I started shooting cooking videos of simple, easy, and delicious foods that I prepared. People started reaching out and telling me that my products were the answers to their boring diets.

People across the country asked me to write recipes and shoot videos for specific low-carb programs. Major diet companies asked me to contribute to their websites, help them develop cookbooks, and help people on their programs. The response was incredible.

My methods and the preparations weren't at all complicated. Instead they were creative, enjoyable, and took a fraction of the normal time. Best of all, the results tasted delicious. Sure, we experienced a few failures here and there. In no time at all, though, I had accumulated hundreds of recipes and began sharing them with family, friends, and people online.

As interest ramped up, I started producing products once again. Before long, I had a little warehouse and shipping center set up, and my kids became masters at stuffing boxes and slapping on postage labels.

I assembled a variety of cooking kits to make it easy for people to cook delicious foods on their programs. Some were for general healthy eating, and some were for specific low-carb meal programs like Medifast, Advocare, Weight Watchers, etc. Others were for people who just wanted to jazz up their cooking. Regardless of the specific needs, my products worked for them with amazing results.

The feedback that I continue to get to this day is unimaginable. My inbox stays flooded with emails of gratitude and thanks, of success stories of weight loss, health battles won, and happy, fulfilled people whose only goal was to make a satisfying meal.

By 2012, my products had been sold in all fifty states, Canada, Ireland, Scotland, and Australia. Undoubtedly, people needed help. They wanted answers. They needed a role model, and they wanted to get rid of the guilt and stress.

Most of all, they didn't want to feel alone. They wanted a community that understood the burden they carried of not feeling like they cared for themselves or their families. They wanted a way out, and more than anything, I wanted to give it to them. No one else could offer to the world what I could.

The old beliefs and notions about myself, that I wasn't worthy of success, of love, and of acknowledgement became less important (although not eliminated). Everything in my life was showing me that I was worth so much more than I ever realized. I began to finally believe that I did deserve the things that were coming my way.

Putting myself and my needs first and taking the risks of divorce and facing life on my own had all proved to be monumental in my newfound state of bliss.

By taking responsibility and action, I had made quality decisions that were really paying off.

10

BELIEVE AND RECEIVE

"Don't limit yourself. Many people limit themselves to
what they think they can do.
You can go as far as your mind lets you.
What you believe, remember, you can achieve."

—Mary Kay Ash

Before long, my life and my business shifted
dramatically.

The plan I had created was coming to life. With my
sights set on the future, and my heart finally over the anguish
of divorce, I was finally ready to make a huge leap, and the
doors seemed to be opening.

After twelve years of joyful living in our big old house, I put
it up for sale. The kids and I decided that a fresh new start in a
new home in a new neighborhood and going to a new school
was in order.

I desperately wanted to downsize our seventy-five-hundred-
square-foot house and its ten acres that had been my marital
home. I wanted to move into a smaller, newly constructed
house, something that was all mine and where I could start
fresh.

The kids looked forward to new friends, a new school, and a new neighborhood. The time had come for some pretty big changes, and we were all ready.

When I finally received the right offer for my house, I accepted it. The kids and I found a new home in an adjoining neighborhood, and I signed the contracts to purchase it that same week. Fortunately, it was vacant, so it provided some flexibility for my plans.

Then life got even busier. Over a period of six months, I became so frantic with all of the paperwork for the house sale and accompanying attorneys, realtors, packing, movers, new school enrollment, kids' new schedules, and getting the new house ready that I could barely think.

I also had to figure out what to do with all of the *stuff* that had accumulated in my house during the last twelve-plus years. My ex-husband wanted barely anything from it. So to add to my tasks, I put together the whirlwind yard sale of a lifetime and watched as memories walked out the door for pennies on the dollar. It made me sad but also excited about what lay ahead. While difficult, that was one of the most cathartic days in my life as I got rid of the old one item at a time. By end of the sale, I had a pocket full of cash, pretty much an empty house, and my eyes set on a new start.

During those few months of transitioning and packing, I functioned on overdrive, going through the motions. I worked off my daily to-do lists, trying to get ready to move while some days barely keeping my head above water.

When I look back on all that I had accomplished during that time, I'm not quite sure how I actually did it while holding myself, the kids, and our household together. Somehow, though, I managed to get everything all done. I proved I could be Wonder Woman if I really needed to be, but I knew it was the last time I ever wanted to be that strong and autonomous again.

My sense of independence and what that really meant in terms of a meaningful relationship began changing along with my journey of self-discovery. In breaking free of the destructive codependence with my ex-husband, I was free to explore new relationships and new ways of engaging in them.

I had dated on and off in the two years in-between the divorce and the move, having many wonderful experiences with men and creating some lifelong friendships in the process. One man in particular stood out from the crowd.

In the spring of 2012, I met an incredible man through the magic of online dating, and we became inseparable. His presence not only provided me strength physically and mentally, but he showed me love, adoration, acceptance, encouragement, and joy like I had never known.

His masculine leadership, honor, and respect proved to be just what the kids and I needed and wanted in our lives and so much more. He was instrumental in the physical move between homes as well as in the mental move that set me and my children free from our old thinking patterns in regard to men, women, and relationships.

In no time at all, he became a significant part of our family life. He was an amazing role model for my kids and for me. In him I found peace and inner strength. In addition he gave me the self-confidence I had needed in my life as well as the reassurance that I was beautiful.

Where the window man had unleashed my quest to be feminine, my new man had taken me to the next level. He revealed the hiding goddess in me by appreciating everything about me without judgment or question. I was accepted and worshipped for who I was and was asked to be nothing more. I was perfect in his presence. It was a feeling I had never experienced.

He was a tremendous help, and there was nothing he wouldn't do, from fixing a doorknob to moving furniture to picking up milk for the kids on his way to the house. If not for him and his presence on so many levels, I don't think I would have survived. More importantly, his mental strength and emotional support gave me the courage to keep moving forward.

Once again, I was forced to put my new business on hold during the move. I was simply too exhausted to handle anything else. Besides, I honestly wasn't really sure what to *do* with my new company, which at that time was called Time Savor Solutions. I had grown it as much as I could on my own and knew that if I was going to do anything more with it, I would need some help.

I had dreamed it would become a big company, but I had no clue how to get it there. After the move, I hired two business consultants to assess it and give me suggestions as to how to take it from a hobby to the real deal. Although I had shipped product around the globe and was making a little bit of money, it was not enough to support me and my kids for the long haul. In addition, I knew deep down in my bones that so many people needed my help and that the business could, in fact, be huge.

I have to honestly say, though, that I still didn't actually believe I could own and operate much more than a hobby business. I was just a single mom. Why would I think for one minute I'd know one thing about growing a successful company? Besides, if I gave all that time and devotion to it, what would I have left over to give to my kids? I needed to pick one baby or the other, right?

My business advisors, however, came to a more optimistic conclusion. They had crunched numbers, completed marketing analyses, and evaluated every nook and cranny. They blew me away when they told me I had a phenomenal concept that was ripe for the picking in the marketplace, hands down. Their numbers showed that the company could be worth millions of dollars in just a few years.

Moreover, they concluded that I was just the woman to make it happen. My on-camera presence, my product line, and my cookbooks and recipes were unlike anything else in the marketplace. They truly believed the name Stacey could and should be just as recognizable as the likes of Rachel, Ellen, Martha, and even Oprah. I was astounded (not to mention scared).

My tribe of customers and followers were proof that I and the business were destined to do great things and help millions of people in the process. The numbers showed phenomenal growth potential over a short period of time. Both of my advisors suggested I go for it.

I couldn't believe my eyes or ears. I panicked with fear yet allowed myself to get swept into the rush of excitement. Instead of being true to my gut feelings (something I would learn *not* to ignore over the years), I got stars in my eyes, figured I could handle whatever came my way, and dove right into everyone else's plan.

Impulsively I told both of my advisors to do whatever it took to move forward full steam ahead. Then for the next six months, I put all my time, all my energy, every available penny, and every second I could into building what I thought would be my dream business.

I spent hours and hours on the business, doing everything that was needed. I wrote recipes. I balanced my financial books. I attended potential investor meetings. I shot videos. I developed products and whatever else was needed from me.

I still tried to be a mom and a girlfriend, but in my heart I knew I was failing miserably in those roles. I started to get angry and resentful that I couldn't seem to get ahead no matter how hard I pushed or how I was advised, and I was exhausted. Deep down inside I knew something was very, very wrong. While I couldn't put my finger on it at the time, looking back now I can clearly see the cause of all my misery.

While I was given all of the numerical evidence I needed to *prove* the business could and most likely would succeed, while I had a team in place, something didn't sit right.

The biggest missing piece of the puzzle was *me*. My heart just wasn't in it. I did not in any way, shape, or form actually *believe* I could successfully run, manage, and handle the business while also living a purposeful and happy life.

The old story I told myself over and over again had taken root and sprouted from deep inside of me. Without any rational thought, I had emotionally assumed in my heart of hearts that no matter what I did, it would be a colossal failure. Someone would wind up with the short end of the stick. There was no way I could have it all without letting someone down in the process. Yet I continued going forth because I was too afraid to tell my consultants "no," and I was too afraid to let down my kids, my man, or my family.

My phenomenal team of advisors, my amazing man, my then ten-year-old daughter and thirteen-year-old son, my friends, and others in my family had been behind me one-hundred percent. While they were huge cheerleaders, I was in total fear.

I was in fear of not being able to handle the growing business around me. I was afraid it would consume me and keep me from being a mom. I was afraid I wouldn't have time for anyone or anything else but the business. Most of all, I was petrified of disappointing everyone around me when it all came crashing down.

I ignored my gut and my fear, and in no time at all, I had a direct sales team of over fifty people working for me. I had a top-notch consultant in the field at the helm who was more than encouraging. I had my kids thinking I was going to be a superstar, and I had a partner saying, "I believe in you. Honey."

On the flipside, I also had mounting financial obligations and business debt to pay back.

I continued to be scared to death, afraid to tell everyone what I really felt. I was too fearful to just stop the forward momentum, even though I knew I was at a pretty serious personal breaking point. I was exhausted mentally and physically, and its effects started to impact my life.

My relationship with my man had become very strained because I was all work and no play. My kids suffered from lack-of-mom time and were becoming too independent at too young an age.

I was heavily invested, using every cent to hire my advisors, create a team, and make a plan. In spite of it all, it was not panning out as I had hoped.

Not wanting to give up, I met with a few more venture capitalists, but in no time at all I knew that neither I nor the business were ready. I was stuck in a typical catch-22.

The venture firms I met with told me that I needed to prove the concept of the business better and that I needed to be more successful, increase my sales, and have more interest before anyone would give me any money. Yet I needed funding to do just that.

There was nothing more I could do. Inside I felt like a total failure.

I tried to keep a smile on my face and faith in my heart that the business could organically grow without any additional investment, that we could make it on our own. While I was hopeful on the outside, I was doubtful on the inside. In the early stages of enthusiasm, I had bitten off more than I could chew. It was too much, too soon, and I just wasn't ready. I didn't believe *I* could be a success, and much like Henry Ford said in the quote I referenced earlier, I proved myself right. I believed I couldn't do it, and so I didn't.

Pretty soon I ran out of what money I had left. I hit brick walls that couldn't be scaled, and I knew I had to tell the team we were ceasing operations. I felt devastated but also relieved.

I pulled my sales team and my consultants together for a meeting and told them that I could no longer support them and that I needed to stop doing business as usual. That meant no more direct sales force, no more consultants, and no more team. I needed to simplify and go back to an online retail sales model. Since I needed to do away with the direct sales model, they were no longer needed as an independent sales force.

That was the hardest day of my life. I just had to walk away and let it all go. I had let everyone down, and I felt that I had failed myself yet again.

I went home that night and ate a whole pepperoni pizza and drank an entire bottle of wine. I cried through the salty, greasy sensation of it all, wanting to feel nothing but numb.

I eventually passed out from the cabernet and the exhaustion. Needless to say, this splurge only made me feel worse. Now not only was I a failure, but I was a big, fat failure who was a hypocrite to boot. If I couldn't keep my mouth shut and not succumb to my food demons, who the hell was I to teach anyone else how they could?

The next morning I was still in a serious funk. Looking for comfort, I called my best friend. It was a warm sunny day, and I paced my front lawn while we spoke. Not long into our conversation I found myself collapsed on the ground in a fetal position. I lay there cradled in the grass and warm earth crying my eyes out with my friend on the other end of the phone. I was grateful that I lived in a remote area on top of a mountain with no one close by to hear me.

Everything around me had crumbled and indeed failed. My business vision had been completely obliterated. Additionally, my wonderful man, who had become so much a part of my world, had notified me during the previous week that he was done with our relationship and was leaving me.

The stress of the business combined with my not paying attention to him and the negative impact it had on our relationship were too much. I was devastated. I had no team, no money, no business, no man, and no hope. Everything I had worked for, everything I loved, everything that meant the world to me had vanished.

I was mentally and physically wiped out after all I had been through and truthfully only a day or two away from checking myself into a mental hospital. I knew that something had to give and that I needed time to heal. I had tried to be a superhero, and I needed to admit that I wasn't, and I needed to be okay with that. I had failed in achieving what I thought the prescribed "goals" were. However, I knew in my core that although I might have failed in the tasks I had tried, I personally was *not a failure.*

When I look at the situation now, I see how things could have been drastically different if I had had the ability to simply be vulnerable and open up to my man and my advisors about my fears. I was so afraid they would be disappointed if I changed my mind about the business direction and if I didn't follow their plans. If I had been authentic and true to myself rather than trying to make everyone else happy, things might have been different.

I could have told them about my reservations, that I was scared, that I needed to slow down, and that I needed to create a business plan that was parallel to my wants and desires and to my life. But I didn't.

I was afraid that if I didn't do what I was told by my advisors, that I would be a failure. Regardless, failure came in the end.

It was the same in my relationship. Through my silence I had sabotaged my relationship with my man in the same way I had sabotaged my business. In fact I had pretty much driven my "Mr. Right" away with my actions of worry and guilt about being seen as less-than perfect. Sure he had his flaws like everyone does, but for the first time in my life I had *exactly what I wanted*, and I threw it all away because I didn't want anyone to see me so unsure of myself after I had come this far. I couldn't reveal this side of myself, not even to the one man I could trust more than anyone in the world.

I was still, however, in such a bad place that I found myself turning to food for comfort. One night in particular, not long after I lay on the grass, there was a turning point.

I had been standing in front of the fridge with a stick of pepperoni and a box of cookies. Still feeling unworthy, I was clearly numbing with food. A few bites into it, I realized what I was doing and found the strength to simply stop and put everything away. I then walked out of the kitchen. Some part of my brain was able to make me aware of my habit before it led to a full-blown binge.

The next day I was able to reflect on the magnitude of that wake-up call. I acknowledged that the day before I was actually able to recognize when I was on the verge of a binge, and I was able to stop myself. I was getting stronger. Wanting to develop that "muscle" that had prevented me from my binge, I became willing and open to the possibility that I maybe, just maybe I had more control over my food issues than I ever believed.

In my quest, I asked everyone I knew for suggestions. Conversations with my friends during this time led me to read some amazing books. I wanted to uncover the truth about my limiting beliefs, the negative stories I seemed to keep telling myself, and how much they had held me back. The power of belief is simply amazing, and I knew I could harness it positively.

In his book *Think and Grow Rich*, Napoleon Hill wrote, "Whatever the mind can conceive and believe, the mind can achieve." Never was a statement more true and applicable than in my situation. (On a side note, this book can change your life, and I highly recommend reading it.)

While I knew that thinking good things could bring good results, what I didn't realize was that the reverse is equally powerful. When you think negatively, you can't help but to attract negative things into your life. When we think bad things, we can make bad things happen. I had done just that.

Now I can honestly say that what I consider to be the lowest point in my life, which was the day I was curled up on the lawn *feeling* such despair, had to happen. It *needed* to happen so that I could understand my limiting beliefs and how I was the one who kept myself down in my comfort zone where I had learned to play small. This held true not only with my business but with my intimate relationships and my weight and body images as well. Unlocking these limiting beliefs was the answer. Lying at the bottom left me with only one place to go—up.

I started to see that I did not *have* to be a superhero to be a success. I could be just me. I needed a break to regroup, to pause, and to *just be.* I had learned to be honest and vulnerable with my few close friends, but I needed to learn to be vulnerable, open, and honest with myself and others in business as well. This mindset included learning how to stop giving so much of myself and begin to receive, trusting that the process of doing so would provide me with what I needed.

I pretty much walked away from all aspects of the business. I still had spices for sale and did a few things here and there to keep customers happy, but I needed distance from it. I then went out to get a J-O-B to support my children and myself.

The time away gave me space to breathe, to collect my thoughts, and to further my journey of self-discovery. I wanted to look at myself and my life differently. I wanted to wake up and discover what it meant for me to live a purpose-filled and happy existence. I wanted to be authentic to myself, to figure out who I was, what I wanted, what kind of physical body I could really be comfortable in *(did I really need to lose any more weight?)*, and what I wanted to actually be when I grew up. The world was my oyster, and rather than looking at it as a bottomless sea of despair, I began to see wonder and opportunity.

I started to take classes on attaining happiness and personal peace at the School of Practical Philosophy in Wallkill, New York. I hired a life coach and got into a routine of taking classes, visiting with my coach, going to work, and playing with my kids.

I kept it simple. I read more articles, watched YouTube videos, and listened to audiobooks on healing and understanding. I took a weeklong women's retreat in the hills of Tuscany and had the time of my life. I spent a few thousand hours immersing myself in learning how to better understand me and how to improve my self-confidence and how I fit into the world. I accepted that being happy was simply enough.

The lessons I took away from "all" of this work were really not complicated in the least bit. To get what you want out of life, all you need to do is feel worthy and deserving, to *believe that it is possible, and take the action necessary to make it happen.*

There's no magic to this. A book or guru can't advise you how to do this or tell you why you need to do it. It's solely up to you. You either believe you can have it, or you believe you can't. Whichever way you decide, ultimately you'll be right.

I had reached a point in my life when I wanted to start feeling worthy again. One year after I began my journey to find me, I knew my purpose lay in my mission to help others feel whole, healthy, and worthy. I knew that my business was the way to make this happen. I knew that the time had come to transform the mess my life had become into the message of hope it was intended to be.

The time had finally come for me to fly.

11

THE FUTURE IS NOW

"Our human compassion binds us the one to the other –
not in pity or patronizingly, but as human beings
who have learnt how to
turn our common suffering into hope for the future."
—Nelson Mandela

W hile the journey of self-discovery never has an ending point, I knew I was ready to bring my message to the world. I now felt confident and at peace.

I was certain of my purpose in life and how it manifested itself in my business. I finally felt comfortable enough in my own skin to forge back out into the business world again. My belief in myself skyrocketed.

My little family had settled into a happy routine, and we were doing well. My kids thrived at school, and I happily worked my nine-to-five job, or so I thought. While I enjoyed my job because it provided a steady salary, benefits, and comfort, I knew I wasn't reaching my full potential.

I had been keeping in touch with my tribe of mommies from the old neighborhood and made a point of meeting with them occasionally, although our kids had grown well past the playdate stage. I had lunch with one of these friends. In the normal course of conversation, she asked how I was doing and if I had ever thought about bringing the business back to life.

I excitedly told her about how I wanted to relaunch it once again. However, I was a little afraid of what people would say and if this time around, I would successfully be able to balance home, work, and life.

My dear friend stared directly into my eyes from across the table. "I have always believed in you, admired you, and looked up to you. If anyone can make it happen, *you* can, Stacey."

I thanked her for her words and went home that afternoon with a sparkle in my eyes and a spring in my step.

A part of me had been reawakened, thanks to that interaction. Once again as before, by making a really scary choice to reveal my true self to a friend, to allow myself to be vulnerable and admit that I felt things I didn't understand, my life started on a new course. Sharing my insecurities gave me the validation I needed to take action.

The exposure felt scary, but you know what? My friend was thrilled that I had told her this. She not only *wanted* to help and support me, but during our lunch she shared similar stories of times when she had felt the same way. Hearing her story was not only comforting, but I felt honored that she told it to me and gave me the opportunity to support her in return.

I reflected upon something I had heard from Brenè Brown, author, speaker, and all-around-awesome expert. In her TED Talk titled *Listening to Shame*, she shares her research findings. "When it comes to raising critical awareness and increasing our resilience to shame, the most powerful words we can hear are: Me too, you're not alone."

The empathy we get and give is powerful, connecting, healing, and inspiring. It's not to be feared; it's to be embraced. That's the power of being vulnerable.

Our lunch turned out to be so much more than soup, salad, and laughs that day. It gave me the final push I needed to get out of my comfort zone and the simplified life to which I had returned.

I revisited the business, and I slowly got back into the game. Rather than just plowing ahead this time around, I got serious. I needed a team. I needed a plan. I needed to treat my business like a business and to start acting like a business owner, not as a hobbyist dabbling in spices.

I knew my perception of myself and my business would determine the eventual success or failure. The time had come for me to step up to the plate and swing with confidence. What I believed, I would achieve. This time, I was going for the moon.

I hired Kristin Tabbert, an amazing business coach from the 12 Week Year program (Kristin@12WeekYear.com), and set goals and deliverables for myself. I wanted to share with the world my dreams and plans and most of all my messages of hope, inspiration, and healing through food. I would no longer be playing small in my life, and I made the determination to hold myself accountable.

Through a happy set of circumstances (although I will tell you that I truly believe there are no accidents in life), I met a wonderful woman who would become my best friend and business partner.

For one year, we worked tirelessly to put all of the pieces of the Stacey Hawkins brand puzzle back together. We successfully earned financing through the Small Business Administration and moved forward full-steam ahead. While our lack of experience, naiveté, and blind faith caused us to lose quite a bit of money to a less-than-scrupulous big-city firm, we learned lessons and created a strong foundation upon which the brand could grow.

I also thrived personally as well. The time off that I took to *find myself* was paying off with huge returns. My relationship with my children was stronger than ever. I went back to eating right and exercising, losing the weight I had put on from my stressful eating. Blissfully I had even rekindled my botched relationship with Mr. Right.

Physically I felt fantastic, but after the several-year journey of losing over a hundred pounds, I stared at my body, loving what I had done, but unhappy with what I saw in the mirror. The years of being overweight had done its damage on my skin, and I wanted a change.

After a consult with a handful of plastic surgeons, I opted to have surgery to remove some of the excess skin from my body and to physically put me to where I had always dreamed. The surgery was unnoticeable to anyone who didn't see me in a bathing suit, but it was transformational to me.

My outside now matches my inside, and while far from airbrushed perfection, it is perfect for me. I truly love what I see and how I feel. The surgery was a great gift I gave to myself. I am so grateful to my doctor, to my amazing man who so lovingly took care of me during recovery, and for the supportive network of people around me.

My new outer appearance only served to reinforce my growing self-confidence and self-worth. Combined with the change in my mindset, the change in my body convinced me like no other that it was time to bring my message of hope to the world in a big way through my work.

Soon, the Stacey Hawkins brand of products, messages, and philosophies had been rebranded with clear, compelling lessons of hope and encouragement. My amazing business partner and friend had an opportunity to start her own marketing company, and we parted ways knowing that the time was right for us to go off on our own. I also knew that the time had come for me to hire a big team to springboard me forward, and this time I was ready.

The book you now hold in your hands is a result of my collaboration with an amazing team that is helping me bring my inspirational story of hope and joy to the world. I know as you read it, many things may have resonated. Hopefully you have laughed, you have cried, and you have come to understand that you are not alone in this world.

I personally know how valuable it is to have someone who shares your story and with whom you can trust and find encouragement. I know the power that these kinds of relationships can have, and I am both honored and grateful that you have given me the opportunity to be there for you like so many of my advisors have been there for me.

I also discovered how incredibly powerful the act of forgiveness is and what a critical role it plays in the ability to happily move forward. After years of working with my advisors, I was able to clearly see how my mother, my father, all the people around me, and even my aunt simply had done the best they could in their lives and in their actions toward me. While the decisions they made *did* have a tremendous impact on my life, everyone simply did the best they knew how. I have made peace with that and no longer harbor anger or resentment for their decisions.

When we know better, we can do better. Therefore, I am grateful for these experiences, and where there is gratitude, there can be love. To forgive and have accepted the fact that situations are simply what they are have allowed me to have stronger, better relationships with many of these people, especially my parents. More importantly, they have allowed me to experience a stronger and better relationship with myself.

Before I conclude, I want to share a story that I remember in great detail. On a sunny afternoon, not long after I started fantasizing about my business once again, I sat in the office of Sheila Pearl, my life-and-relationship coach.

During a casual conversation, I shared with her my fears about life and business, how stuck I felt, and the transformations I wanted to make in all of my relationships for the better. As I started to talk, I could feel the tension move up to my throat.

In no time the tears rolled down my cheeks. I said, "I can't do this."

She asked, "Why?"

I hung my head down and answered her one-word but very crucial and applicable question in a quiet voice. "Because I'm not supposed to."

Her eyebrows furrowed as she asked sweetly but sternly, "Says who?"

"I don't know," I replied. Then for the first time, the good girl in me made a profound admission. "I need permission."

She gave a huge smile, and her wise, seventy-year-old-plus blue eyes twinkled. "Aha!" she blurted as her hands flew up into the air.

Then she gently took my hand as she focused her eyes on mine, and her smile faded. Her voice was soft yet her tone was serious when she said, "I give you permission to live the life you want to live and to do whatever it takes to get there. Now give yourself permission to do the same and soar."

The pit of fear in my stomach disappeared. With her simple words, my wish to live my own life had been granted. I had the desire, I had the belief, and I had the action plan. Now I had the permission.

We often feel the need for permission to move forward with anything scary because it provides the much-needed encouragement and liberation we need to seek our truth. We look for external reinforcement when we want to do something risky and when we want to push outside of our comfort zone with no guard rails and no net to catch us. We want someone, something to reassure us that we're going to be okay and that we're making the right decision. We want to know that someone is going to be around to catch us when we fall.

I want you to take that little flicker of hope and excitement that you feel in your heart (because I know it's there) and hold onto it. Most importantly, I want you to see that no matter how difficult your situation is or how hard or challenging it may seem, you have the power to do, to be, and to have anything you want.

As I discovered, it takes some work, but the rewards can be abundant. In doing "the work," I discovered the truth and the understanding that is the key message in this book—the world and the people in it are truly not conspiring against us; rather, we conspire against ourselves and deny ourselves happiness as a result. We can find peace and bliss in trusting that the world is really working in our favor.

When we open ourselves to new possibilities, we see opportunities for happiness and freedom from burdens, whether they're struggles with food, with relationships, or with ourselves. We simply need to want them, believe we can have them, and take action to get them.

The same holds true for those in our lives whom we blame for our circumstances. We blame our parents. We blame everyone else for making us feel bad, worthless, and less than, and we blame our past. The truth is that no one can "make us" feel anything. We make ourselves feel the way we do.

People who have left us feeling hurt simply need to be forgiven. We must remember that we are all doing the best we can.

What is important is staying focused solely on your own journey, not anyone else's. Remember that you are worth everything the world has to give you. It is of the utmost importance that you remain grateful in receiving all that it serves up.

If you believe yourself worthy and if you are willing to take action and do the work today, what will your life be like tomorrow or one year or ten years from now?

You have the power to be the author of your own life and to write (or even re-write) your own story. You can shine your own light, and you can achieve your dreams and reap the rewards you never before thought possible. The power to do so lies solely in your hands.

Right here, right now, I am holding your hand from afar, looking into your eyes, and giving you permission to start writing the story of you with all of your beauty. You have a light to shine and a great purpose in the world. It's up to you to live fearlessly and find it.

I give you permission to dare greatly, to dream a *huge* dream, and to create a healthy, empowered life free from struggles with food and self-hatred.

You are worthy of that life, and I look forward to celebrating with you and nourishing you, bite by bite, every step of the way.

Resources

Business Coaching

Kristin Tabbert
K.L. Tabbert Performance Coach
Certified 12 week year coach
www.12weekyear.com
www.12weekyearcoach.com
Kristin@12weekyear.com
989-786-1122

Life and Relationship Coaching

Sheila Pearl, MSW, CLC, Relationship and Life Transitions
Coach
Author of "Ageless & Sexy: The Magic of Sensuality"
www.SheilaPearl.com
info@SheilaPearl.com
845-542-6057

Sexuality, Pleasure, and Relationship Consulting

Pamela Madsen
Founder Back to the Body Retreats for Women
www.PamelaMadsen.org
Pamela@backtothebody.org

Weight Loss Consulting

Take Shape for Life / TSFL
Paula Martino
Information link: http://www.whatistsflmartino.gr8.com/
Email: paula@free-coach.com
Phone: 845-430-9590

Advocare
Liz & Jesse Cort
https://www.advocare.com/120724601/
Lizcou23@aol.com

Breakthrough M2 Weight Loss & Wellness
Nannette & Brian DeGroat
www.breakthroughm2.com
info@breakthroughm2.com
845-713-4320

Ketopia
Tom & Kim Challan
Website: http://getketopia.com/
Phone: 760-855-4002
Email: tomandkimchallan@gmail.com

Education & Inspiration

The School of Practical Philosophy
www.PhilosophyWorks.org
Branches located throughout the world

ABOUT THE AUTHOR
STACEY HAWKINS

Stacey Hawkins is an author, speaker, and international entrepreneur who admits that success takes work. From hosting taste-testing parties in her kitchen to taking her product line around the globe, Stacey is driven to help others reach their potential. Using her real, everyday, and approachable strategies for staying connected to personal health, happiness, and what matters most, her inbox remains full of testimonies from those who have used her tactics and succeeded.

STACEY HAWKINS

Stacey has published five cookbooks and her how-to memoir *Too Big for My Britches: How I Let Go of Body Shame and Became Proud of Simply Being Me (and How You Can Too)*. In telling her story, she doesn't hold back, using her own life experiences to share the realities and challenges of stress, family commitments, guilt, shame, and the desire for a balanced life. Stacey delivers not only the message of hope of attaining health and happiness, but she provides practical, everyday methods to turn wishes into reality.

Her dynamic personality shines throughout her speaking engagements, and as such, she is a much sought-after motivational speaker, engaging audiences of all types and sizes. Stacey is the former television host of *Real Meals with Stacey Hawkins*, and she now appears in numerous cooking videos on YouTube. She has also made numerous appearances on television and radio shows.

Stacey's articles and recipes have been published in many newspapers, journals, and magazines, including *Success Magazine*, and her blog The Stacey Hawkins blog at www.StaceyHawkins.com is read internationally. Her recipes have helped thousands on the Medifast / Take Shape For Life diet program and as such, the Medifast Corporation sought her expertise in the creation of their cookbook *The Lean Green Meal Cookbook*. Her passion has caused her to help thousands of people adopt simple, healthy, and stress-free eating and living habits as her products continue to sell throughout the United States, Canada, United Kingdom, and Australia.

In addition to filling the roles of employee, employer, entrepreneur, and single mom trying to balance it all, Stacey is acquired the prestigious title of professional chef at the Culinary Institute of America and is recognized by the American Culinary Federation as a Certified Culinarian.

Stacey has a living laboratory in her blended family of children, spouses, ex-spouses, and pets, crazy schedules, jobs, and everyday obligations. Every eating and lifestyle strategy, as well as every recipe gets tested in her own life first and only the best make it to her platform. She currently lives in New York where outside of work and creating tasty and delectable spice concoctions, she spends her free time with her two children.